I DON'T HAVE TIME

First published 2017

Exisle Publishing Pty Ltd
'Moonrising', Narone Creek Road, Wollombi,
NSW 2325, Australia
P.O. Box 60–490, Titirangi, Auckland 0642,
New Zealand
www.exislepublishing.com

A CiP record for this book is available from the
National Library of Australia.

ISBN 978-1-925335-32-3

Designed by Tracey Gibbs
Typeset in Avenir LT Std.
Printed in China

This book uses paper sourced under ISO 14001
guidelines from well-managed forests and other
controlled sources.

10 9 8 7 6 5 4 3 2 1

Disclaimer
While this book is intended as a general
information resource and all care has been taken
in compiling the contents, neither the author nor
the publisher and their distributors can be held
responsible for any loss, claim or action that may
arise from reliance on the information contained in
this book. As each person and situation is unique,
it is the responsibility of the reader to consult a
qualified professional regarding their personal care.

I DON'T HAVE TIME

15-Minute WAYS TO SHAPE A LIFE YOU LOVE

EMMA GREY & AUDREY THOMAS

EXISLE PUBLISHING

'This book spoke to me from the very first page. Finally, a time-management book for real people by real people. It was interesting and engaging with stories and anecdotes that made me laugh, cry and nod my head in agreement. If you only read one self-help book this year, make it this one.'

Alison Abernethy

'THE "MY 15 MINUTES" PROGRAM HAS RE-AWOKEN MY PASSION FOR LIFE. I DIDN'T EVEN REALIZE THAT I HAD LOST IT AMID THE DAILY GRIND, BUT NOW I HAVE SO MUCH MORE ENTHUSIASM AND ENERGY.'

Beth Cavallari

'Thanks so much! Some simple things that we forget, and the reminder that we need. And fantastic ideas we'd never think of. Loved the program!'

L.K.

'This book has it all — laughs and tears, advice and support and, most of all, the encouragement most of us need to just get started! Learning how to make the most of the smallest chunks of time has made a huge difference in what I achieve. Thanks for the inspiration!'

Alison Bailey

'I knew I would like this program from the moment I read the description! The biggest thing I have taken away is that now if a task seems insurmountable, I think "I'll just spend 15 minutes on it". It's a mindset that can help everyone.'

Anne George

'THIS PROGRAM IS AMAZING AT REMINDING YOU HOW MUCH IS POSSIBLE AND IT ONLY TAKES 15 MINUTES AT A TIME. IT RE-ENERGIZED AND RE-IGNITED ME AS AN INDIVIDUAL, SETTING ME ON A NEW PATH OF SELF-DISCOVERY AND SELF-WORTH WHICH BENEFITS EVERY ASPECT OF MY LIFE.'

J.L.

'The storytelling style of this book made it unique in the genre for me. There are few traditional time-management books that provoke regular tears and "ah ha" moments the way this one did! Thoroughly recommended.'

Sarah Turner

'I am completely impressed with Emma and Audrey's professional and personal style of supportive coaching. They have profoundly changed my life, my outlook, my beliefs about myself. I am a stronger, more confident person at home, work and in my relationships with others. I feel this and others close to me have noticed, too.'

Fiona McIntosh

'LOVED THIS BOOK! A PAGE TURNER FROM START TO FINISH WITH AUDREY AND EMMA'S ENGAGING STYLE OF WRITING CONVEYING THEIR RELATABLE STORIES.'

Michele Farrell

EMMA GREY is a work–life specialist who uses a suite of innovative concepts and tools to provide organizations and individuals with practical solutions to the modern challenge of 'having it all'. Emma runs seminars, workshops and executive coaching, writes regularly for national media, and together with Audrey, is co-founder of the highly successful 'My 15 Minutes' program (www.my15minutes.com.au).

AUDREY THOMAS is an experienced coach and facilitator with a background in project and change management, learning and development, and operations management. After a corporate career spanning the UK, Europe and North America, she now specializes in working with individual clients and teams to discover and develop their untapped potential and improve effectiveness.

TO OUR PARENTS
FOR GIVING US ALL THE TIME IN THE WORLD

AND TO JEFF
FOR THE PRECIOUS TIMES

CONTENTS

I NEED MORE TIME!

BY ABIGAIL TURNER, AGED NINE

My name is Abigail and I am in 4P.

My topic is 'I Need More Time' and you may be wondering, for what?

Well, to do my homework, eat chocolate, ride a horse, go shopping.

I think we should have 48 hours in a day and 24 hours for a night.

But the downside would be longer school hours, longer homework, longer time your parents have to nag you. It would take a longer time to eat your breakfast and you would get to school late every day …

Then you would get shouted at by the teacher because the teacher doesn't like you being late. More time in the world would mean more time sitting in the dentist's chair and I already sit in there too long as it is! And what if more time meant having to wait longer for your cake to bake in the oven? Oh no! That would be a disaster!

But, on the upside, if we had twice as much time each day and night, you would have more time to see your friends and travel to meet people in other countries. And another really good thing if we had more time is there would probably, and hopefully, be fewer wars in the world because people would have more time to get to know each other, and understand each other. Then maybe we wouldn't have wars because there wouldn't be anything to fight about.

And what about me?

Personally, if I had more time, I would do all the things I love most in the world:

→ Go on the computer
→ Go trail riding every day after school with my favourite horse Sooty
→ Drink my favourite cookies-and-cream milkshake at Oliver Brown
→ Go to Fiji on a holiday
→ Watch *How to Train Your Dragon* all day
→ Play netball
→ Climb every tree and wall I can find
→ Go shopping for toys and books, especially books, and lots of toys too
→ Make models with my dad
→ Play ninjas with my sister in the backyard; and
→ Go for walks with my mum, without my sister!

What's that you say? I'm out of time? Oh dear, *I need more time!*

INTRODUCTION

WHY SUCH A RUSH?

Emma:

I tried not to think about the ravenous parking meter as I perched for six hours on an unforgiving plastic seat in the arrivals hall at Canberra airport. My then fourteen-year-old, Sophie, and her best friend were hoping to catch a glimpse of American YouTuber Colleen Ballinger. Colleen's alter ego, the hapless 'Miranda Sings', has a cult following so fanatical her madcap spoof on self-help books was propelled to the top of the *New York Times* bestseller list a mere 24 hours after its pre-launch. Perhaps I was quietly fangirling about that too …

We knew Colleen had performed at the Melbourne Comedy Festival the evening before. We knew she was scheduled to perform in Canberra that night. The missing detail was which flight she'd be on, which is why we'd found ourselves at a virtually empty airport just after dawn.

The girls were resplendent in Miranda's trademark costume: a men's striped shirt tucked into red track pants with 'Haters back off' emblazoned on the rear, clashing pink Crocs and too much red lipstick. I was dressed normally and held onto the first of several strong cappuccinos, hoping that this wouldn't be a wild goose chase. Quietly lurking in a security-rich environment for hours with the teens decked out as identical nerds, clutching glittery posters, was bound to attract attention. The girls were stared at, photographed by tourists and even approached by the police at one point.

'Who are you waiting for?'

'Miranda Sings.'

'Who?'

Exactly.

Eventually, in the early afternoon we reached a point where we just wanted to go home. At least I did. It was reminiscent of the transition stage of labour. I honestly couldn't do this any longer. I wanted an epidural.

Turning to Facebook, I hoped to be galvanized by messages of support from my friends. What I received instead was more along the lines of: *'Five hours?* Are you crazy? Who has time to waste doing this on a Sunday? Don't you have better things to do?'

I did have other things. But were they better?

Somewhere in the sixth hour we turned our bloodshot eyes towards the arrivals gate for the umpteenth time. Were we hallucinating? Or was that *her* (wearing a normal amount of lipstick and normal clothes)? As the escalator conveyed the online superstar towards us, along with her then fiancé (also a famous YouTuber) I sent a silent prayer to the Gods of Social Media and Celebrity Chasing: *Please take a second to stop and say hello!*

The automatic glass doors parted. She glanced up from her phone, saw the girls, broke into a smile and went straight into their arms with the type of hug usually reserved for long-lost friends. Then she introduced us to her sister (another YouTuber), posed for photos and promised to follow them both on Instagram. When you're fourteen, and you've been waiting six and a half hours to meet your online idol, an Instagram follow *is your life*.

But this story isn't about any of that. Not really.

Fast-forward a few weeks, and the same two girls were upset when I collected them from school. A friend's mum had developed worrying symptoms of memory loss and confusion. She hadn't recognized her own child. The likely diagnosis was early-onset dementia. In her forties. My age.

That was the moment for me. I thought back to the hours we'd invested in our loopy airport adventure and knew with unwavering certainty that I wanted to spend *more* time hanging around arrivals lounges with teenage fangirls. Not less.

> Everything changed the day she figured out there was exactly enough time for the important things in her life.
>
> Brian Andreas

HERE IS OUR PROBLEM, IS IT NOT?

We live in a time and culture where exhaustion is a status symbol. If you're not frantic or flat out — if you don't have too much to do and not nearly enough time in which to do it — eyebrows are raised.

'How have you been?' someone asks.

'Busy!' you chirp, because it's the only answer you've ever learned to the question. 'How was your weekend?'

'Need a holiday just to get over it!'

'Gah!'

'Insane!'

'Crazy!'

'Ludicrous!'

'Actually, everything's cruising along quite calmly,' nobody interjects, ever. 'Work's under control. The house is organized. Had a date with my partner on the weekend, and devoured two novels …'

Eh?

Crazy schedules!

Ships passing in the night!

Me-time? Ha.

That's the game! None of this freewheeling about lackadaisical weekends and under-control workloads and free time and romance! This isn't a gap year.

Women of a certain age and stage have decided we're officially swamped, as a species. One does not simply *swim*. One *splashes* dramatically in a sea of largely self-inflicted over-commitment, despite people throwing lifebuoys and yelling that you can actually touch the bottom if you just stop struggling and stand up.

'HURRY SICKNESS'

Author James Gleick refers to what he calls 'hurry sickness' — that feeling of being trapped as we lament the hectic jobs (which we applied for) and drive the kids to a barrage of after-school activities (which we signed them up to) that we squeeze around second degrees and diplomas (which we enrolled in) as if the whole shebang is not a circus of our own making. Even when we do have breathing space, the story we tell tends to be one of being time-poor, stretched and tired. Because that's the story that is valued in our society. It's the story over which so many of us bond — sometimes for hours, while we soak the sponge of our precious time in circular conversations about how *there's never enough time …*

Lean in. Lean out. Push. Pull. Sprint. Collapse. The awkward choreography of modern life jars against the rhythms in our health, relationships and careers. We crank up the sound until it grates and we can't hear the music any more. We keep spinning across the stage, even when our bodies ache and our minds churn. We dance, not because nobody's watching but because we're worried that everyone is.

And right there, in the midst of too-full lives, jam-packed with 'shoulds' and 'musts' and 'I wish I hads', there are our Miranda Sings moments. There's the colour that's been dimmed or missing from our lives. There are the things we really want to do, and we want to do them *now*, regardless of what else is happening and what people think. There's a state of peace achievable not just during rare breaks away from our normal lives but in the midst of them. And there are the cherished dreams we've swept under the carpet for 'one day' when things are easier and less hectic, and there are fewer people clinging to us.

HOW DO PEOPLE DO IT?

So, I say raise your expectations.
Elongate your process. Lie on your
deathbed with a to-do list a mile long
and smile at the infinite opportunity
granted to you. Create ridiculous
standards for yourself and then savor
the inevitable failure. Learn from
it. Live it. Let the ground crack and
rocks crumble around you because
that's how something amazing grows,
through the cracks ...

Mark Manson

There's no special secret to chasing your dreams, and no secret 'productivity sauce'. People who've shaped lives they love haven't hacked the system or found a magic door into a parallel world with twice as much time, where everything always comes up roses.

The sparkly world of social media tricks us into thinking there's a genetically modified breed of Deliriously Happy People who've somehow slipped through the reality net and appear to be leading super-sized lives. Always smiling. Always winning. Always hitting goals amidst a flawless regime of self-care and posting motivational quotes to prove it. #nofilter #blessed

We're not talking about the tiny percentage of people whose airbrushed perfection asserts itself from the pages of glossy magazines. It's not the people basking on yachts in designer bikinis, sipping Verve Clicquot from Waterford crystal flutes, that are really the challenge for us here.

It's the woman next door. The one with the up-to-date curriculum vitae and tidy car, whose kids seem biologically programmed to manage more than one spoonful of breakfast cereal without a choreographed fanfare from a marching band. Or it's the woman above you in your Facebook news feed, the one with the partner or babies or career or family life or holidays or home or financial security or hobbies you crave. Or the one with *all* of that, tied in a bow.

It's tempting to gaze longingly at the lives of others, wishing we knew their secrets. Tempting, and dangerous. Because, if your neighbour doesn't have a breakfast-cereal problem, she'll almost certainly have a problem in the bedroom. Or the boardroom. Or the fitting room. There will be some 'room' in her house — some window of her seemingly Class A life that is shielded from public view — from which she gazes longingly at the life of the woman next door, or the one below her in the news feed ... *wishing she knew your secret.*

> Lives we love aren't sculpted by stomping darkly through our minds in steel-capped Doc Martens, kicking ourselves each time we don't measure up. They're shaped when we tread lightly through our mess, treating chinks and fractures with a homemade balm of humour-scented self-compassion.

We have to stop worrying what other people think and get clear on what *we* think. Clear on what matters most — to us. From there, it's a simple matter of just getting on with it. Right?

Well, it might be simple, were it not for the relentless chatter in our minds, telling us we don't have time, we're not ready, we can't be bothered, it's too late, it won't work or we'd rather be doing something else.

'Adulting!' Who knew it would be this tricky?

CONFESSION ...

It's the third day of January, and we're three days into the serious resolution we made to chip away at a little part of this book each day from now until we're contractually obliged to deliver it to our publisher in six months' time. Which means we have six months (minus three days) to squeeze 50,000 words around all the other things: our jobs, families and any unforeseen challenges that may crop up in our lives.

It seems doable if we tackle it methodically. Thus far, though, *hmm ...*

On Day One, we opened a new Word document, typed the heading and changed the font to Helvetica. On Day Two, we had good intentions, but spent the afternoon on Netflix watching a documentary about the Backstreet Boys and redecorating a child's bedroom respectively. No matter! We thought we'd get around to book-writing in the evening. But didn't.

It's now Day Three, and the first day we've actually sat down and done what we committed to do — which was simply to 'get on with any bit of it'. No excuses.

What stopped us until now (and we're not just talking about those three days, but the previous three months since we signed the contract) was a serious case of 'overwhelm'. After all, there are days when we struggle to churn out a 600-word blog post. A whole book seems a hefty thing.

It's like any long-term goal: substantial weight loss, a long course of study, spring-cleaning the house — at the beginning it has the look and feel of Everest. And we've had the look and feel of people who've made it as far as Base Camp and now have a lovely publishing contract to show for our efforts, plus a blank Word document with nice Helvetica headings that we're seriously considering swapping to Verdana because it's super-important to invest several days getting the formatting just so.

It hasn't helped that Emma is co-writing a musical based on her teen novel with a composer friend from school. Staying up late swapping lyrics and song ideas is fun. Writing the musical based on an existing book seems *easier* than starting this new one, so there's a war waging: 'Must do the harder project. Might throw together a few lyrics first.' Hours pass. A song is written, and another day goes by with massive progress in the area with no deadline or contract and nobody to let down if it doesn't get done. 'We can't leave this till the last minute!' we say to each other. 'We can't pull an all-nighter to produce a 50,000-word manuscript.'

Getting the contract for this book was the single most exhilarating career development for us both last year. It meant the publisher had faith in our ability to offer something fresh in the field of productivity and self-improvement. It gives us an opportunity to share the stories we love, and expertize and ideas that it's taken us years of work and study to build. One of the reasons the publisher placed that trust in us is because we're hired by some of the world's top companies to lead people to thrive professionally and personally. Our online programs have attracted thousands of busy people seeking help to manage their lives.

Another reason we were asked to write a book is because we tell it like it is. At a work–life presentation for a 'big four' accounting firm a few years ago, an audience member came up afterwards and said, 'I nearly didn't come. I thought you'd be these impossibly together, stick-thin figures preaching about your seven-step system to get this stuff right … and it was refreshing to see you're not like that *at all!*'

Oka-ay!

Just quietly, there are days when we feel like the Jennifer Saunders and Joanna Lumley of the time-management field. While others are doing the 'top ten things that all successful people do before breakfast', we're stealing '5 more minutes' and wrangling school lunches in our pyjamas. You won't find us walking over hot coals to master our mindset. You'll find us stumbling over Lego, and lots of it, which is arguably more courageous.

There's a motivational style that's big on eternal optimism and relentless reframing and overcoming. It works brilliantly for some. Others are left wondering what they're doing wrong when they inevitably find themselves having days where optimism goes AWOL. Days where they don't want to 'reframe'. They just want to 'sit' for a while as disappointment or sadness or fear washes through them.

No matter which tools we use to accomplish what we want to get done, the reality is that 'life' happens. Our glorious, complex inner 'human being' emerges.

KINDSIGHT

There are times when we glance around, desperately seeking a grown-up to fix our situation or tell us what to do and we're horrified to realize there is no one ahead of us in the queue. We're up! All we really want is to have a proper meltdown or run away, and we're urged to 'manage our state' or write gratitude lists or meditate. These are immensely helpful techniques, but techniques that are easy to ignore in rebellious, human moments, when our 'better judgment' appears to be sitting this one out.

That's when we need to deploy bucket-loads of what author Karen Salmansohn refers to as 'kindsight'. That's hindsight with kindness, because there isn't a person amongst us who isn't doing the best we can, with what we have, where we are, knowing what we know at a certain moment in time. We're doing all of that with a unique cocktail of external pressures, laced with success and failure in different measures.

The two of us are proud of what we've accomplished and how we handle things a lot of the time. We achieve things in our lives, careers and families that feel really important and valued and fun. Our glasses are almost always half full. We are dream chasers. We make some great things happen that bring us and other people joy, and we have lots of exciting future plans.

But it's not all sunshine. We mess things up. This book isn't intended to offer an unrealistically upbeat approach with little tolerance for the 'crunchy' days that end in tears (our own), when we scramble over the finish line and flop into our beds wondering where the day went and what we did wrong. We share our deepest failures openly, as normalizing what's hard is half the battle.

Bridget Jones said, 'It is a truth universally acknowledged that when one part of your life starts going okay, another falls spectacularly to pieces.' While writing this book, other parts of our lives and careers inevitably flailed in the manuscript's wake. It wasn't pretty, but we took comfort in J.K. Rowling's perspective: 'People very often say to me, "How did you do it? How did you raise a baby and write a book?" And the answer is I didn't do housework for four years. I am not superwoman! Living in squalor — that was the answer!'

People rarely achieve anything worthwhile
without skinned knees and grass stains.

It's not about trying to work out which things will turn to gold if we touch them. It's about learning to let go of our attachment to specific outcomes as we go out and *meet* life. It's about hugging opportunities to our chests, particularly the opportunities that seem just out of reach and make us feel a little shaky.

Audrey:

It's also about laughing it off when that shakiness causes us to stumble, spectacularly.

I was starting work with a new client and it had been 'one of those mornings' on the home front. Still, I'd made it out the door. I was heading in the right direction for my appointment and feeling very grown up while I was on the phone to Emma, catching up on some business things — relatively well-prepared and organized, despite the chaos with the kids.

As I was driving, and talking, I reached to adjust my necklace, and that's when something quite horrific occurred to me.

'Oh, my God!' I said to Emma on the phone.

'What?'

'I can't tell you!'

'What do you mean you can't tell me?'

I felt sick. *Sick!*

'Emma, I've forgotten to wear a bra,' I admitted, not believing the words that were coming out of my mouth.

It would be nice if I could say she was sympathetic to my plight, but I was almost deafened by her roaring laughter. Here I was, stuck in a traffic jam, heading into the first of several corporate workshops for a new client (wearing a figure-hugging jersey top, I might add) with *no bra!*

Who does that? How? More importantly, how was I going to fix it? I could see a Target store across several lanes, but calling in would make me very late. Late, but respectable. It was my only option.

'What am I going to tell the client?' I asked Emma, while I hurtled into the car park.

She was too busy taking notes about the story as it unfolded. Apparently forgetting to wear a bra while presenting a high-level leadership workshop was a perfect example of embracing our imperfections. I ended the call and fronted up (in more ways than one) to the Target lingerie attendant and said, urgently, 'I've forgotten to wear a bra and have a workshop to present in 40 minutes. I need to find one, change into it and buy it. In that order. Please help me!'

She looked at me as if she understood (what a lunatic I was) and helped me swiftly complete my mission, except that when I went to the service counter my accomplice was nowhere to be found.

'I'm buying a bra,' I announced to the teenage girl on the counter, 'but I'm already wearing it. I had a ... wardrobe malfunction.'

She nodded and said she knew all about it. Everyone knew, I was sure of it. Emma had probably blogged about it while I was still adjusting the straps in the fitting room ...

As I walked into that training room (in the most comfortable bra I've ever owned, might I mention) I wondered if I was *ever* going to get my act together.

WHO IS THIS BOOK FOR?

This book is for you if you're a real person, battling a voice inside that tells you way too often that, 'You can't' or 'You'll do it later'. Or 'You need more time'. It's for you if you're 'not ready' or 'not good enough'. It's for you if you're consistently putting other people first or deferring precious ideas, or thinking 'I'll be happy when ...'

You *can* do it. Whatever it is.

And you can do it now.

You have all the time you need, no matter how 'busy' you are. We promise.

This is not a flashy, seven-step system to achieving your goals, unveiled by stick figures. It's a collection of down-to-earth true stories interwoven with practical tips — presented as experiments, or what we like to call '15-minute magic' — to help you use your time the way you really want to. It's a plan to help you drop the excuses you're making for not getting on with things that really make a difference. This book is built on a premise that it's possible to ditch the notion that there is not enough time. It's possible to actively shape lives we love by paying attention to what matters most, even if it's just for 15 minutes, or 1/100th of our day. What matters is the time we spend doing meaningful things that we love, personally and professionally. What counts is creating slices of magic in our lives with people who really matter, while we can. *I Don't Have Time* will help you do just that.

If we can call ourselves out on the ways we get in our own way — the habits we entrench, the fears we shrink from, the actions we repeatedly take that move us further from what we crave — we can move ourselves to a fresh starting point. This is a place of true honesty, where our excuses for not starting or not pushing through when things are hard, fall away. A place where our cover is blown. A place where the choices we make that over-fill our days, or that siphon minutes and hours and days and months, even *years*, into a void of wasted opportunity, are exposed.

It's about the battles we're waging not with 'lack of time' but with something else: overwhelm, disinterest, boredom, disorganization, lack of direction, anxiety or fear, rebellion or any of the other genuine causes for our slower-than-desired pace or stagnation. And this isn't only about making gung-ho progress on our biggest goals. It's about making time to surrender, release and rejuvenate, too. It's about each of us bringing our unique collection of important things to centre stage.

HOW TO USE THIS BOOK

The first chapter of this book, 'I'll be happy when ...', is about mindset and where we're coming from. It's a platform to swim out to and catch your breath on, before we dive into the five themes we've chosen. Each theme represents one of the mindset 'gremlins' that tangle our thinking. You won't make every excuse we've listed in this book, but you will gain an appreciation of just how much untapped power you have over your use of time.

Through the practical, 15-minute experiments we'll show you how simple it can be to make a small difference in your day. Those daily differences can snowball into a much more satisfying life in a short space of time.

Everything you need to make some simple changes right now is contained within these pages. We've also prepared some bonus resources, including videos that will deepen your engagement with the concepts in this book, which you'll find at www.my15minutes.com.au/bookbonus.

Get real, and you'll find you *do* have time. Fill that time with things that move you forward in areas that really colour your life, and you'll start to hear the music again.

WAIT!

Don't read another word until you've stuck your feet in a bucket of warm water.

Seriously.

Maybe you're reading this on a train. Or you're at work in your lunch break. *Are we mad?* You can't just strip off and plunge those feet of yours into a bucket of water in front of your boss! Or perhaps there's a toddler clambering on your lap as you try to read this sentence for the twenty-eighth time. Maybe this book is being batted away by a copy of *The Very Hungry Caterpillar* or you've just sat down for the first time today and now we're asking you to get up again and organize to stick your feet in a bucket — have we taken leave of our senses?

Yes, perhaps we have. Perhaps we all have. We spend so much time dashing through frantic lives, dropping things, clambering, that many of us *have* taken leave from the very sensory experiences that have traditionally helped to ground and calm us:

Bare feet on freshly cut grass.

Sunlight twinkling through leaves.

Sand between our toes.

We want this to be more than just a book. We want it to be an experience. Let's call it 'actual reality' (like virtual reality, but real). It's where you get to experience bonus extras in little experiments as we go through the chapters, starting with this one over the page.

Fill a bucket with warm water and grab a towel. Add some of those unopened bath salts, body wash or bubbles that loiter like wallflowers up the back of the bathroom cabinet waiting for 'one day'. Or add a cup of Epsom salts plus a cup of apple cider vinegar. Or if you're out of all that, add nothing. Sit down for 15 minutes with your feet swishing in the bucket of warm water and *stay there!*

Nope, not doing it.

Sometimes, the only bubbles you'll notice are the ones made by your own excuses as they rise to the surface, asserting various reasons why you can't stick your feet in a bucket, as simple as it sounds, probably followed in quick succession by, 'This always happens! I can't even do the first task.'

The 'My 15 Minutes' approach is about gently overcoming our natural urge to put things off at the slightest hurdle. It's about challenging the self-talk that gets in the way of us pushing through obstacles, the 'I'll do it later' promises we make to ourselves without following through. This experiment is not about recreating the ambience of a five-star retreat, but about sitting down, slowing down and taking care of yourself — where you are, with what you have, for only a few minutes. If that means doing it with a toddler beside you splashing in a different bucket, do it. If it means doing it when you get home instead of now, do it. If it means doing it with plain warm water and no bubbles, do it. If you don't have a bucket, use the bath. If you don't have a bath, up-end a storage container and use that.

If you do this experiment and you inadvertently kick the container over on the tiles and it saturates all the presents under the Christmas tree, then you'll have recreated an unfortunate accident one of us once had with a homemade foot spa. Sometimes things don't turn out the way we imagine. Maybe you'll settle down to relax and your baby will wake up or the tweens will start squabbling, or your partner will walk in after a bad day, oblivious, and start ranting about the guy at work. This stuff happens. But not 'every time' as we sometimes convince ourselves, mid-whine. Sometimes, when we give something a go and the experience is thwarted, part of us gives up. Bit by bit, we abandon the idea of making life nicer for ourselves because 'it's too hard' or 'it never works'. What we tell ourselves then is a story that chips away at our potential fulfilment. It's a story we don't have to buy and one that we have the power to change.

YOU MIGHT BE WONDERING

Isn't this process of shaping a life I want meant to be about pushing myself out of my comfort zone and doing brave stuff fearlessly? What's fearless about sticking my feet in a bucket? Can't you challenge me with something big instead?

Chasing a different life and taking risks to make things happen always starts from a place of deep self-worth. Reaching for what we want often means running a gauntlet of obstacles, both real and imagined. Without a solid belief that, 'I deserve this' it's tempting to let those obstacles get the better of us and watch our dreams slip away.

When we've spent a long time being swept along in a current of 'all the things' — nurturing everyone else first and struggling to keep our personal 'show' on the road — prioritizing our own dreams and ambitions can seem too hard. One of our friends discovered this when she embarked on a university course in her forties, posting this on Facebook:

After another week of distractions and disruptions, having still not caught up on my university reading, I am today starting the assignment which is due in a week. I'm wondering whether it's all worth it. What purpose does this study serve? Is it worth the stress of trying to fit even more deadlines into my busy life? I'm starting to think that, as much as I want to do this, it's just going to end as it has before, with me deciding that it's easier/less stressful to simply prioritize other people and activities rather than focusing time and energy on studying, which seems like a self-indulgent choice at the moment.

A few weeks later, having persevered, the same friend received her first assignment back with a high distinction. We were so pleased that she hadn't surrendered when it had seemed too hard — when fear of failure and succumbing to others' needs or wants had almost tempted her into self-sabotage.

FIRST EQUAL

It doesn't take much to knock us from the branch from which we're trying to fly. When we fall from our perches, as we naturally will while we find our wings, clambering back to that launching point takes some effort. We're only going to put in that effort if we truly believe we are 'first equal' in our lives, and that our goals are worth striving for.

If we can't prioritize something as crucial as our self-care, and if we can't learn to let everything and everyone else go and 'just be' for 15 minutes, then sticking with the bigger goals you'll be encouraged to set later in this book will be that much harder. When you do take a few minutes for a personal indulgence, it's worth paying attention to what goes through your mind. If the chatter is about what we 'should' be doing, and if our minds are darting around to-do lists, frantic about this 'wasted time', then Houston, we've uncovered a problem we need to work through.

If you've let self-care slip, then making this little piece of pampering your first practical step towards boldly claiming the life you'll love is a gentle way to experiment with the concept of 'acting as if'. It means you can give yourself permission to do something regardless of not 'feeling it' yet. It's the 'fake it till you make it' notion and, in this case, it's about acting as if you deserve this 15 minutes of me-time, even if your mind is whirring rebelliously against the idea of prioritizing yourself in this way. Ralph Waldo Emerson said, 'We are always getting ready to live but never living.' Stopping for 15 minutes is a reminder of what 'living' can feel like, particularly if your default state is 'preparing'.

As we move through the following chapters we describe some of the thoughts that cause us to choose inaction over action, invariably leading us into shaping a life we *don't* love — a life that bores or irritates us, one that brings us down and makes it even harder to get motivated. We've made this fun, tangible and life-changing, in steps that are completely manageable, with just a little commitment to follow through. So please, get up and arrange that bucket of water now. You'll love it!

We invite you to jump onto social media and post a likely unglamorous pic of your tired feet in a bucket with an upturned copy of our book on your lap, and the hashtag #Idonthavetimebook like this is the grown-up woman's answer to the Kylie Jenner Lip Challenge. This is not just about spreading the word about the book (but thank you for doing that), but about keeping yourself accountable and helping other readers who search the hashtag to find images of people following through on this small action. Even in the smallest of ways, we shape our lives not by *imagining* how nice it would be to do things like this, but by getting on with it.

I'LL BE HAPPY WHEN ...

Happiness makes up in height for what it lacks in length.

Robert Frost

What does it really mean to create a life you love? We know it's not about perfection. There will always be light and shade. It's not about trying to nail down the emotional butterfly of 'happiness'. It's not having a life free of disappointment, failure or heartbreak, and it's not just the children's movie *Inside Out*, which captures the notion that there's a valid place for all emotions. Social researcher Hugh Mackay expressed it like this:

> ... the idea that everything we do is part
> of the pursuit of happiness seems to me
> a really dangerous idea and has led to a
> contemporary disease in western society,
> which is fear of sadness. Wholeness is what
> we ought to be striving for and part of that
> is sadness, disappointment, frustration,
> failure; all of those things which make us
> who we are.
> Happiness and victory and fulfilment are
> nice little things that also happen to us, but
> they don't teach us much.

Learning to embrace the full rainbow of emotions is a start in creating a life we love, and there are other ways to measure how satisfied we're feeling in our lives.

WHOLENESS, PACE AND GROWTH

There's a meme from cartoonist Cathy Thorne that depicts a woman with speech bubbles above her head. 'I love routine,' she says. 'Until I'm bored. Then I love excitement. Until I'm overwhelmed. Then I love routine.'

We tend to feel stimulated and 'alive' when there's room for excitement, passion and variety, but not *so* much activity, difficulty and adrenaline that we feel like Sandra Bullock in *Speed*. According to author Tom Senninger we tend to hang out in one of three places:

→ *The comfort zone*, where we feel safe, stable, secure and unchallenged (and also a bit bored and lifeless after a while). It's like a sunken lounge lined with oversized cushions, chocolate and best friends. So enticing! But spend too long there, and you start going a little stir crazy.

→ *The learning zone*, where we're excited, challenged, expectant, exhilarated and 'alive'. This is where things are stimulating without being overwhelming. There's enough 'new' and enough 'challenge' to keep us energized by the sense of growth.

→ *The panic zone*, where we're stressed, frustrated, annoyed, anxious, fearful, tired and fed up. There are times when we'll inevitably enter this place due to external events or because we've taken on too much, or taken steps far beyond where we feel sure-footed. We can survive here for a while. Going through periods of higher stress is normal, and our bodies are designed to cope with this.

Following is a list of possible criteria for leading a life you love. Thinking about your own life over the past few months, how many of these relate to you?

- [ ] You leave space to think creatively.
- [ ] You're excited about things that you're doing.
- [ ] You feel motivated and inspired.
- [ ] You love the variety in your life.
- [ ] Several of your activities are very satisfying.
- [ ] You make time for enough sleep, you fall asleep easily and sleep well.
- [ ] You make time for exercise and eating well.
- [ ] You have regular 'down time' with friends, family and on your own.
- [ ] You say 'no' confidently.
- [ ] You think before you accept a new task or role.
- [ ] If you take on something new, you take something old off the list.
- [ ] You spend some time being 'still'.
- [ ] You're free of 'guilt' or a sense of obligation.

- [ ] You're comfortable with the pace in your life, and the pace has variety.
- [ ] You have just enough pressure for a 'buzz' yet not so much that you feel stressed or overwhelmed.
- [ ] You feel that you have many choices.
- [ ] Most of the time, you're in the driver's seat of your life and you choose the speed and direction.
- [ ] You take regular, proper holidays and use some time on weekends to wind down.
- [ ] If your favourite author launches a new book, or your favourite artist drops an album, you can easily stop and enjoy it.
- [ ] You're organized, insofar as you don't waste a lot of time searching for things.
- [ ] If something new and important crops up, you have the capacity, energy and space to deal with it.
- [ ] You laugh a lot.
- [ ] You have good, long, relaxed conversations with the people you love.
- [ ] When you go to bed at night, you feel satisfied with how much you have achieved and positive about what you'll do tomorrow.

Let's not be Pollyanna about this. There are times when something strikes us from left field and we enter 'survival mode' to get through it. Sometimes we get stuck in survival mode for longer than necessary, because a stress haze descends and our perspective gets clouded. However, meeting as many of the conditions listed above as you can, as much of the time as possible, *will* make for a more satisfying life. Luckily, that kind of life isn't lived on a perfect pedestal from which it's easy to fall and hard to struggle back onto. It's a living, breathing, adaptable lifestyle that you walk through, tweaking as you go.

This is something we're both continuing to learn and finesse the older we become and the more 'experience' we plough through. That experience comes either purposefully, because we've chosen something, or because we find ourselves having to dig our way out of something we didn't plan or want but find ourselves facing anyway.

Living a whole and stimulating life, at a pace that feels great most of the time, is the way of living for which we strive. Yet there was a time when we fell a long way short of it.

WHO AM I TO THINK I CAN DO THIS?

You gain strength, courage and confidence by every experience in which you really stop to look fear in the face ... You must do the thing you think you cannot do.

Eleanor Roosevelt

We didn't just wake up one day, confident enough to write a book or start the business that preceded it. In fact, there was a time when neither of us would have imagined we'd be in the position we're in now to be working on these things.

It's a confidence continuum. Just as an eldest child will always push parents into fresh territory as 'first timers', the next step up in other parts of our lives seems daunting, no matter how much experience we tuck under our belts. Often the people ahead of us seem *way* ahead of us. While there are things we work on now that we feel comfortably competent in and confident about, there's also all this 'new' stuff! It's exciting, terrifying and confusing. Because the moments where we want *so much* to step up and outwards into something new and big seem to waltz with moments where we don't want to do those things *at all* — where it's more attractive to retreat to the safety and security of a quiet life with little risk.

It's worth connecting the dots between your earlier experiences and the way you tackle things now. Whether or not we're consciously aware of it, we're all getting through the world driven by a set of beliefs about how the world is and how *we* are — some of which are resourceful and lead us to great things, and some of which hold us back.

If we don't question the beliefs that drive us, we can become like an elephant tethered to the spot by a small chain pegged to the ground. The elephant stays stuck because it learned as a baby that it wasn't strong enough to pull away from the peg holding it. Eventually it gave up trying. Years of conditioning gave it the belief that it was trapped, despite its growing strength.

When we tell ourselves that we're trapped in a situation and can't move on, change or make different choices, often we're pandering to the expectations of people who hammered a peg into the ground and chained us to it when we were too young to understand that one day we'd be strong enough to break free. Or we're trapped by our own misunderstanding or misreading of a situation in our past, failing to entertain other perspectives. We can be unaware of our own strength and potential, trapped only by our mindset, standing incredibly close to the freedom we desperately long for.

Audrey:

'You've got to be kidding!' I remember thinking when I read a story in our local newspaper about a woman who was being hailed a hero in our community. Beaming out of the picture on the page was the teacher I'd had when I was seven, whose words had unknowingly shaped how I approached life from then until I was nearly 40 years old.

I'd always considered myself to be really lucky when it came to my career and business pursuits, maybe even blessed with some kind of magic workplace fairy dust because I was always in the right place at the right time. 'Synchronicity' was definitely on my side. I always fell into ideal-for-me job opportunities. Rarely did I consider that perhaps it was *me* who was ideal for a job. How could I be? There was no way I was smart enough for any of these roles!

It's a story I'd been telling myself since I landed my first 'grown-up' job in retail banking when I was just sixteen. I enjoyed my work and was keen to learn, even if I believed I 'wasn't as bright' as the other office juniors. Later, egged on by friends, I applied for a role in a brand new department, never expecting to get it and, at twenty, I was surprised to be promoted to a classification level that usually would have taken several more years. It was blind luck that got me there, too. I was sure of it. I worried that someday, someone was going to find out that I really wasn't very smart at all.

At 25, I was appointed into an operations management position in the bank's call centre. Despite winning the job on merit, it was a bittersweet achievement. The more responsibility I took on, the more in the spotlight I would be. I couldn't hide my lack of intelligence in this role: 'They are going to catch me out at some point. They'll work out that I can't do this, that I'm just faking it.'

A few years of 'faking it' later, and wanting a break from a leadership role, I took an opportunity for redundancy and a lower-level temp job in a recruitment agency, but it seemed my 'miraculous' career wouldn't be contained. Within a few months I became a recruitment consultant and then a specialist call-centre account manager. Being promoted well above where I thought I'd fit, I was just waiting for my career to come crumbling down around me …

After four years working in recruitment, I left Australia to travel to the United Kingdom for what I anticipated would be a sabbatical year. I planned to fund some travel around Europe by working in a pub or doing some temp assignments for an agency. But, apparently, being a 30-year-old backpacker is not my thing, and within a few months I started in a role within a large corporate organization. Yet again, I'd fallen on my feet.

The luck didn't stop there. Less than 18 months after starting with the company, I found myself leading a global team of learning and development professionals, working on the project which was to shape so much of the rest of my corporate career. I regularly travelled and worked in the United Kingdom, North America and Europe and was thoroughly immersed in the career I thought had simply landed in my lap, through my remarkable knack of being in the right place at the right time. For years I told people that the reason I got the job was because one day I wasn't concentrating in a team meeting, and my boss delegated the training portfolio to me. Just another lucky break — being the only one with training experience in the room at the time!

After six years I excitedly moved back to Australia with my Welsh husband, Dafydd (Daf), expecting our first child. Again, I was 'lucky' to land the perfect family-friendly role in a company doing some consulting and training work. And again, despite being told that I was a valuable member of the team and being paid well, I had a familiar thought lurking in the back of my mind: 'Why are these smart, business-savvy people paying me for consulting services? Why do they want my advice? If only they knew how very un-clever I am!'

We all have defining moments when something happens and we make it mean something important and form a core belief about ourselves around this. Back in Year 3 at school I was a bit of a chatterbox. I enjoyed social interaction much more than my school work, and this didn't impress my 'old school' teacher, the local hero featured in the newspaper. Sometimes she would make me stand in the corner facing the wall or, worse, send me out to the corridor and exclude me from class activities. A chatterbox I may have been but I was mortified at being thought of as a 'naughty girl' and I dreaded being seen out in the hallway during class time by our school principal.

Things got a whole lot worse one evening, when I attended a parent–teacher interview with my parents and sister, Michele (who, incidentally, never got into trouble for anything at school). As was customary on these nights, I sat in the corridor feeling a mix of anxiety about what my scary teacher would tell my parents about me, and excitement because we were in the school grounds at night, when we would normally be home in bed. As I waited, I listened intently for any nuggets of feedback from the other side of the door. My eavesdropping resulted in hearing my teacher explain to my parents something that would go on to inform my self-perception for decades: 'She will be lucky to even make it out of primary school.'

Wow.

I don't remember how my parents responded or where the conversation went next. I was stuck in that moment and I decided to believe this: I was dumb. Other people would always be smarter than me.

I held this belief close to me for many years. How could I not? A teacher, who knew *everything*, had said so. She had decided my fate and from that I naively took my cue.

Interestingly, when I've talked with my parents in recent years about this vivid recollection, neither of them remembered the conversation. But that insidious belief became one of the foundation blocks upon which my life was built. It took me into my teenage years and was ever-present as I worked my way through high school. That's when I developed the companion belief that, contrary to my teacher's prediction, luck was on my side. I made it into high school. In fact, in Year 7 I was offered a scholarship to go to any private school of my choice in Adelaide. I convinced my parents not to send me to a private school, with vague pleas about staying with friends. Privately, though, I knew I wasn't 'smart enough' and the school would work it out. Why bother wasting their time? It was an early indication of how incredibly powerful deeply held beliefs can be. Unfortunately, I proved myself right. I 'wasn't smart enough' to do well at high school and I failed my final year, so I applied for the job in the bank.

Throughout my career this story of being lucky rather than smart plagued me in all but one area of my work — leadership training and team development. Coaching and mentoring people felt like a perfect fit. I was in my element — uplifted and energized by helping people see their true potential and take action to achieve their goals.

In 2009, I developed a strong sense that I'd become too focused on making a living (and faking my abilities), rather than on making a difference and investing my time and energy into what felt right. So, with the support of my husband, I embarked on my formal coaching qualifications, and that's when everything changed. The training led me to dig deep and uncover the beliefs with which I had been kidding myself for nearly four decades. That's when I realized just how much I'd focused on my seven-year-old self's confused interpretation of an ill-considered comment that wasn't meant for my ears, shouldn't have been said and, in the scheme of life, ought to have meant nothing to me. These core beliefs — this particular mindset — had caused a lot of pain over the years. They'd made me question myself at every turn. Once I busted through those lies and replaced them with resourceful alternatives, I realized the power of making those changes myself and being able to help others do the same.

I stepped away from my regular consulting work and jumped with nervous excitement into my own business; in full knowledge that *I create my own luck*. And by then, I was armed with a powerful secret weapon ... the knowledge that I am good enough.

Emma:

I catapulted out of university in my early twenties. When my brain stopped spinning from lectures, readings and essays, it came to rest not on the career I'd prepped for, but on marriage and babies. My parents had me late-ish and I wanted my kids to know their grandparents. Motherhood felt right. So, at 24, I plunged purposefully into the slow lane, career-wise.

My public-sector job paid for electricity, food, clothes, shoes and swimming lessons. It was safe and flexible, and the people were lovely. I could do it with my eyes shut and focus on other things. Important things ... or so I told myself, several years into it, having dredged from somewhere yet another morning's bucket-load of fake enthusiasm for my children's sake.

My plan to tread water with my career had been well intended. I was up for low-stress, medium-level responsibility and work–life 'balance'. But, at the end of the day, the extra energy that I'd hoped to plug into motherhood had already been sapped by the effort it took to pretend things were okay and keep my head in the game during working hours — a situation that spreads virally into your private life if you let it. I'd crawl home, exhausted from another day of cruising in a direction that didn't interest me. I'd tell myself, 'I'm in my comfort zone, and that's ideal as a parent.' It wasn't ideal though. And the truth is I wasn't doing any of it well.

Every so often, I'd catch a glimpse of the magic that lies beyond the dependable career zone I'd fallen into. I'd envy the cool stuff that other people were doing. Bold, creative people, who — even with kids, and even if it meant having stop-gap casual jobs while they established themselves — had grass stains on their knees from all the times they'd fallen over, giving a career they were wildly passionate about a red hot go.

My knees were pristine. The longer I clung to the status quo, the less comfortable it became in the fortress I'd built to stay secure and protected. From what? Exposure? Mistakes? Failure? Eventually it dawned that, in my effort to be conservative, sensible and 'family friendly' I wasn't being me.

The 'Am I good enough?' mantra that had blasted through my internal PA system for years was soon drowned by a new question: 'Is this good enough, this "half-lived" professional life?'

The taste of possibility was more-ish and, despite not seeing the big picture yet, I formed an 'exit strategy'. First question: How long could I stay here, miserable in the wrong job, serving up to my kids a poor imitation of the mother they might have if I was being 'all of me'. And would my alternative plan even work? It would mean starting from scratch, and an enormous drop in income. It would mean a sharp rise in the number of times I heard, 'Are you crazy?' Easier to stay in the comfort zone, perhaps.

Except, having opened my mind to another way, I couldn't close it again. I knew that the 'what ifs' would chase me and find me, and taunt me like a school bully while I cowered in the toilets. Frankly, I was cowering in the toilets anyway, hoping to while away another 5 minutes in an endless working day.

Why not run towards what I wanted instead of away from what I didn't want? What was really the worst that could happen?

As I hit 'send' on a resignation email to my boss in 2009 and registered my first business name, WorkLifeBliss,

I felt one part terrified and nine parts exhilarated. Was this really me — quitting my job? The person with no entrepreneurial or business experience, no clue about how to even get into the back end of a website, let alone know what to do with it when I got there? Someone with only beginner's skills in coaching, no training experience, a rampant fear of public speaking (so bad I'd worry for *weeks* ahead of having to speak at something) and no sales or marketing nous?

I was someone with all of that, plus a big dream to make a difference and enough passion and tenacity to stumble through, *finally* scuff my knees and clamber up as many times as I had to, to make it happen.

COURAGE SHOWS UP WHEN WE NEED IT

We don't need courage to laze in our pyjamas, watching reality TV and thinking, 'I wish my life was different.' We need it in the moment we push 'send' on the resignation email or to sign the enrolment papers and register a business name. We need it not while staring at the brochures for the bungee jump but while standing on that platform. Not while flicking through the bridal magazines but when standing at the altar. We need it in our harder moments too: when saying 'no' to a request we can't take on, to a relationship that's bad for us, or to an opportunity that's right for us in every other person's eyes — just not our own.

In the movie *We Bought a Zoo*, the pivotal moment is right at the point of biggest risk. It's that, 'twenty seconds of insane courage' after which 'something wonderful' happens: we buy a zoo, we move overseas, we surrender to love.

It's like when a small child is barnacled to your ankles in tears at the start of school. You just keep showing up. Facing it together, awful though it is. You push through, tweaking the process. Bit by bit, through exposure to disastrous school drop-offs, the drop-offs gradually get easier. The courage required for your child to keep turning up morphs into confidence through experience. Years later, as she ever-so-coolly sashays into the school yard, you think, 'Is that the same child?' Next, it's her gap year and she's waving a passport and boarding pass and there you are, hoping for a backwards glance. Wishing for just a *second* or two of clinging to your ankles before she goes.

Confidence is the *result* of courage — not the precursor to it. And when we do scary things, maybe our kids, our friends, our colleagues and families watch our transformation and wonder the same thing: Is this the same person, the one who stayed safe for such a long time, wings clipped? No longer wondering 'What if?' but 'What next?'

If getting to that point is your goal, what is standing in your way? How can you hurdle the obstacles and take charge of change in ways that don't require great swathes of your time or have you feeling you're being asked to produce a miracle? Can worthwhile change really meet us where we are? Can it slot near effortlessly into the nooks and crannies of our day? Experience tells us it can.

15 MINUTES OF FUTURISTIC EAVESDROPPING

First, imagine you're at a party ten years from now. You've had ten years in which to accomplish some things, to entrench or disrupt habits and to be present in the lives of those you love. Also at the party are the people who mean the world to you — your family or friends, ten years older than they are now. You overhear them talking about you. As you stand there, you realize they're discussing how you've used your time and what you've prioritized. They're being *very frank*, and your heart begins to race.

Now, grab a pen and take a look at the table opposite. In the left-hand column write your 'rave' list. This is what you dearly *want* to hear your people say about you ten years from now. For example, 'She always had time for me' or 'He prioritized his health'. This is the easy part.

Once you're clear on how you want things to be, make a list in the right-hand column of all the things your closest circle will potentially say about you if *nothing changes*.

What I want to hear	What I will hear if nothing changes

Some items might appear on both lists, and those are the things that are going well, which you want to uphold.

If the right-hand list contains some current truths that you'd rather *shift* in the future — as it typically will — think of this as a positive starting point. This exercise may shine a light on some uncomfortable doubts that you've had for a while. That's a good thing, because you're holding in your hands an opportunity to say 'no' to the choices that are costing you deeply, now and in the future. This exercise can give you a chance to stop such discomfort from morphing into longer-term regret, and that's a gift. Embracing new actions, habits and behaviours now means you'll walk in on that party scene in a decade, pause and listen, and your eyes will fill with tears for all the right reasons.

Let's move on now to the first of five 'mindset gremlins' that might be responsible for some of the factors in that right-hand list, beginning with that fear that we're just not measuring up.

MINDSET GREMLIN 1

WHEN YOU THINK YOU'RE NOT ENOUGH (BUT YOU ARE)

In our seminars and workshops we ask participants to jot down, anonymously, what they *really* think about themselves and their performance both at work and in their personal lives. This provides us with a window into people's secret fears and self-doubts. Every time we read aloud lists like this in groups, people respond viscerally: with gasps, and tears of relief that they're 'not the only one'. That's why we're sharing them with you, too.

As you move through the following chapters, we invite you to treat each 'believe it or not' checklist as a barometer of your own thoughts and fears. This first list pertains to beliefs and fears people have shared with us about failure, comparisons and imposter syndrome. This is all about not feeling 'enough'. See if you recognize any of these common secret doubts.

BELIEVE IT OR NOT?

- [ ] I can't keep up technically and intellectually with people at work.
- [ ] People will think that I'm not coping and that I'm a bad parent.
- [ ] I'm scared of not living up to the expectations placed on me.
- [ ] I don't believe it when people give me praise or say I would do well at something.
- [ ] I'm going to be found out!
- [ ] I can't get married in case it fails like the last time.
- [ ] I hold back both in meetings and socially in case I sound stupid or say something wrong.
- [ ] I fear not saying the right thing at the right time.
- [ ] I am not loveable.
- [ ] I am *bound* to fail!

Our wish for you is that, as you read on, you'll begin to feel a little less alone in your inner 'talk'. One of the trainers in our coaching course expressed his relief at hearing the inner doubts of others. 'I'm not the only freak in the room!' he said, and we smiled.

Freeing ourselves from feelings of not being 'enough' opens opportunities that already exist right in front of us. Imagine how things could be if you didn't allow these fears and feelings to stop you. Imagine the things you might accomplish. We'll begin with a 'big picture' reminder of why it's well worth moving past our excuses and getting on with things despite our fears and insecurities. Uncertainty and fear can wrap their tentacles around us, strangling our confidence and causing us to step back from wonderful experiences. When we decide we're unable to risk failure, unwilling to stumble, and when we cave in to those fears, we lose opportunities to pull things off.

And when we pull things off? Well, it makes every single one of our previous misses worth it. It's a lesson we learned from a very close teenage friend as she faced a terrifying illness, with a little bit of magic from a pop star …

A LESSON FROM LONDON

Emma:

It was the end of the Easter holidays when the father of my daughter's best friend arrived on our doorstep and explained that his vibrant, funny, happy fifteen-year-old, Neala, had been diagnosed with acute lymphoblastic leukaemia. We didn't know until we heard her speak about it on the radio a long while after that life expectancy without immediate treatment could have been as drastically short as one week.

When something like this befalls a family you love, it's hard to know what to do. Their freezer was soon bursting with casseroles. We offered to drive the other two children anywhere they needed to go.

I found myself having to focus on the healthy girl of my own, Hannah, who was unwaveringly courageous beside her friend while in the oncology ward (where Neala spent months). After these visits we'd sometimes drive for hours, windows down, music blaring, tears streaming.

Occasionally I'd find my daughter on the phone at 2 a.m. because the steroids gave her friend insomnia and it's lonely (and scary) in a hospital room combatting cancer. I had to cut those phone calls short sometimes, with school the next day and my daughter gradually becoming nocturnal. That was hard.

We all needed something positive to focus on and, for inspiration, we didn't need to look further than the first posters that went up on the hospital walls in Neala's room: One Direction's Harry Styles. Most popular boy in the world. A pop star with twenty-three million Twitter followers. Wearer of many bandanas ... And here was his biggest fan — about to lose all her hair.

Obtaining one of Harry's bandanas didn't seem that

much of a stretch at the time, but that could be because I was living in a fantasy world, literally — I was in the final stages of writing my teen novel *Unrequited: Girl Meets Boy Band*, in which an ordinary girl from Sydney catches the eye of the lead singer in the hottest boy band in the world. So I said to my daughters, 'How hard can it be to get Harry Styles to strip off a bandana and post it to us?'

They felt sorry for their delusional mother, with her obvious lack of a grip on reality. 'A piece of Niall Horan's discarded toast was auctioned for $100,000,' I was informed. 'The official wish-making foundations struggle to keep up with the volume of requests they receive to meet One Direction.'

Right. I could either ditch this crazy idea (because, let's face it, it was a needle-in-a-haystack chance) or it would be game on! In this instance, I chose game on with the accompanying risk of egg on my face.

'Surely we know someone, who knows someone, who knows someone, who knows someone, who knows Harry,' I thought. 'Does anyone know Harry Styles?' I typed on Facebook to my three hundred friends. Nope. Nobody did.

A few minutes later, a friend from primary school sent a private message, saying her husband worked as a floor manager on a morning TV show, and was good mates with the entertainment reporter who had interviewed the band several times ... and she included his email address.

This daisy chain took a few months but eventually resulted in my email being forwarded directly to 1D management, followed by a phone call I'll never forget: 'It's Bronwyn from Sony Music. I've got Harry's headband here for you. Just need to confirm your address so I can courier it to you tomorrow.'

There is nothing quite like the thrill of watching someone who was by then exhausted from months of chemotherapy opening a brown paper package from Sony Music and finding a note saying, 'Enclosed is a worn headband from Harry, for Neala, as discussed.' (I had of course requested it be worn and preferably unwashed, and the girls inhaled the scent of pop star the second they got their hands on it, as did their mothers if we're honest!)

'Harry?' she said, as she tentatively unwrapped the package. '*My* Harry?'

Disbelief and confusion gave way to an hour of joyous fangirling — from Neala and also from her sister and my girls, all of whom were huge fans, and bursting with love for their sister and friend and this little miracle in the toughest of years. Two of them raided the tea-towel drawer and made their own 'Harry bandanas' for the photos. Then they jumped online and found images of him wearing the *exact* headscarf and Photoshopped the images together. We smiled until our mouths ached. We cried. They screamed and jumped around until Neala felt faint and had to sit down.

For one night, we were almost (but not quite, I'm sure, in her parents' case) distracted from the reason we'd come into possession of this item in the first place.

A few months later, Neala met Harry backstage before a Sydney concert. She took along the bandana and thanked him for giving it to her. He hugged her and said, 'That's okay. You needed it much more than I did.'

Harry, if you're reading this book (and, let's face it: why wouldn't you be?) thank you for the little piece of yourself that you gave a once-sick and now glowingly healthy girl in Canberra. But thank you also for the lesson you taught us about reaching beyond our grasp, even when failure seems almost inevitable and when excuses slam into our tentative dreams. Now, whenever one of those out-of-reach scenarios arises, we have a simple mantra: We got Harry Styles' bandana! We've got nothing to lose!

BUT I'M NOT READY

Only put off until tomorrow what you are willing to die having left undone.

Pablo Picasso

We haven't always been 'fly by the seat of our pants' people. We used to have good ideas and ruminate endlessly. We'd 'save' them, dream about them and plan and prepare … but never actually test them, before our eyes were drawn to the next bright shiny object. This pattern meant we were existing in a wildly exciting state of 'perpetual potential', constantly imagining our future success and endlessly thinking, 'This could totally work!' and 'One day we will …' But we never dipped a toe in the actual water, because that kept our dreams pristine and perfect and free from criticism or failure.

We had all the classic signs of master procrastinators, stuck in a deceptively unproductive cycle of 'information gathering'. It's a clever strategy, because what you're doing feels worthwhile. It was easy to convince ourselves that reading one more article, gathering one more opinion or doing one more course was a good way to spend our time. In reality, we were just stalling. Let's face it: it's safer and more fun to think about the successful end result than it is to do the heavy lifting required to get there.

We live in an age of limitless access to both sensible and dodgy information. That's bad news when you couple it with Parkinson's Law: that work expands to fill the time available for its completion. Without a deadline or cut-off point for our preparation phase in any project or goal, we can row our boats merrily along the river of information forever, gathering, planning, thinking, dreaming … anything but actually riding ashore, getting out and *doing something*.

WHY DO WE DO THIS TO OURSELVES?

Information gathering can be an effective strategy to support what's known as 'secondary gain'. This is the hidden advantage you receive by *not* taking action or changing a situation. The secondary gain in not taking action to lose weight, for example, is that you get to eat as much chocolate as you like. The secondary gain in not going for that promotion is that you don't have the added stress of the role. The secondary gain in not addressing a loveless relationship is that you stay protected from the trauma of a break-up. Secondary gain is a powerful, distracting thing, and is often tantalizingly easier and less risky than the 'higher good' and harder work involved in making changes.

We finally broke free of the chains of living in 'perpetual potential' when we first had the idea for our 'My 15 Minutes' program, which we'll introduce to you on page 57. This was really the first time we decided not to overthink it. In fact, we leapt so impulsively into this idea that we registered the domain name for the program while we were still on the phone together in our initial flush of excitement. Within three weeks, we threw a website together from scratch (with a very heavy reliance on YouTube tutorials and a first-name-basis relationship with the help-desk gurus). Twenty-one days after the idea's conception we had designed the program concept, made the site live and hit 'post' on Facebook. Four minutes after we had launched the program we had our first sale. By the end of our short launch period, we'd had nearly 200 people join a program that was as yet untested. It would mean three months of hard work, seven days a week, and more nights than we care to mention working into the small hours to pull the content together and over-deliver on our promises. But we did it.

The next year, after the success of our first foray into working together, we decided to run an online Speaker Series. We were on the phone again (we often are, as we live over 1000 kilometres from each other) when we had the idea of bringing together a bunch of inspiring women and interviewing them on the topic, 'The 15 Minutes That Changed My Life'. It sounded and felt right. While still on the phone, and supervising our kids in their baths, we Facebook-messaged the first person we could think of with an engaging story to tell — author Rebecca Sparrow. Within seconds she said yes, and immediately sent private messages to several of her inspiring friends, two of whom were instantly intrigued and thrilled to participate. We stayed on the phone and registered a domain name for the series. By the time the kids were dried off and in their pyjamas we had three speakers lined up, a domain name, no idea what we were doing and so much excitement we could barely breathe.

We started making a game of it. Who could we reach out to and ask, even if they seemed beyond our grasp? MasterChef winner Julie Goodwin? She'd be delighted. Seven-time world champion surfer Layne Beachley? She responded almost immediately. Soon we had a wonderful line-up of talented women including award-winning Australian country singer Melinda Schneider, UK working parent expert Amanda Alexander, uber down-to-earth politician Katy Gallagher, award-winning classical composer Sally Whitwell, internationally acclaimed body image advocate Taryn Brumfitt, hilarious authors Mrs Woog and Kerri Sackville and a diverse list of women who were unwaveringly generous and open with their stories. Women we wouldn't have dreamt of approaching only a few days before.

The series was picked up in the national media, the Sunday papers, glossy magazines and across social sharing sites. Behind the scenes, we were the proverbial serene-looking ducks paddling furiously to keep up with the monster we seemed to have created.

As we went to make the call to record our first interview with Dannielle Miller, author and educator in the field of confidence for teen girls, we confessed to each other that we were quite nervous. We'd been interviewed a few times ourselves, but had never sat on the other side of a conversation like this. It felt like a completely different skill. At the same time, we were muddling through the technical logistics: How does a tele-seminar actually work? Can we edit these recordings somehow? What about intro music? Is there some sort of set format for a press release?

As jittery as we were underneath, it all came together. Years later, Dannielle said, 'out of *all* the media I have done in my career, your interview elicited the most real me. You were truly gifted at getting at the issue.' Nobody was more surprised by this than us, given the extent to which we'd been 'winging' it at the time.

FEAR OF FAILURE

When someone standing atop a bungee jump platform in a safety harness glances over the edge and says, 'Stop! I'm not ready!', it's not true. Usually they're entirely ready. Everything is in place and there is no further preparation to be done. What they really mean is, 'I'm scared!'

It's an excuse that isn't confined to our thrill-seeking moments. It masquerades throughout our lives as 'I need more time', causing havoc, disappointment and even stagnation — and at its root? It's nearly always fear of failure.

> There is no passion to be found playing small — in settling for a life that is less than the one you are capable of living.
>
> Nelson Mandela

When in 2016 Princeton Professor Johannes Haushofer shared his 'CV of Failures' on Twitter it went viral. 'Most of what I try fails,' he explained. 'But these failures are often invisible, while the successes are visible. I have noticed that this sometimes gives others the impression that most things work out for me. As a result, they are more likely to attribute their own failures to themselves, rather than the fact that the world is stochastic, applications are crapshoots, and selection committees and referees have bad days.' The document lists the degree programs the professor did not get into, the academic positions, fellowships, awards and scholarships he applied for and did not get, the rejections he received from his submissions to academic journals and the research funding he did not win.

It can be so easy to see others' paths as much more linear than our own. Their stories seem crafted by a master plotter with an eye for the big picture, while ours might appear as a jumble of plot threads, woven together as if composed in the dark. It's tempting to choose to postpone or reject the chances we're offered that might lead to the unfolding of a life we'd love. That way we're less prone to the disappointment we imagine is dolloped into our own lives in more generous doses than the lives of others. It doesn't take many face-plants before it seems easier to swallow the notion that it's all too hard, that others' priorities come above our own and that success is best left for the true 'high achievers'.

This is a slippery slope, as we can begin to believe that a deeply contented life, filled with things that really bring us joy, is beyond our reach. We can believe that kind of life is for people with more time, more money and more help. We can accept stories that life is *always* hard and that work isn't meant to be fun, or that success and contentment are inextricably bound to material wealth. We can believe we haven't got what it takes to get where we want to go, or be embarrassed when things don't work out. We can worry they won't, and save ourselves the angst. We crop our ambitions, and our actions, until everything works out — or doesn't work out — exactly as we predicted.

If you've ever visited an English castle, you'll have seen gleaming suits of armour on display. Many are polished and perfect, without a single chink. These are clearly *not* the armour worn by knights in battle but beautifully intact specimens that have been tucked away safely, in glass cabinets, under the watchful gaze of cutting-edge security cameras. Battle armour is meant to be a mess.

> Really chasing success is a risky, uncomfortable business. It tends to be linked with lots of failure. It has to be, because failure is how we find out what works. By failing, we slash through all the dead ends and wrong turns. Once we clear those away, we can see the way ahead: even if the way ahead turns out to be a flashing neon sign reading WRONG WAY GO BACK, steering us down a different path.

Embracing failure is a very different message from the one many of us learn growing up. When we're little, we break things and spill stuff. We get schoolwork handed back covered in red pen and our hearts sink as we learn all the ways we didn't get it right. We're measured on how well we can balance a chemistry equation or do a trigonometry problem or write an essay, even though most of us enter adult lives where we need to know none of these things. Stumble by stumble, failure becomes something to be feared and avoided. Without necessarily giving it conscious thought, we shrink our lives so we can have a reasonable chance of getting things right and doing things well most of the time. After all, in what universe would getting things wrong and doing them badly ever be a positive?

We may not be Ivy League professors and we're not at the 'pinnacle' of our careers yet, but we were both inspired by Professor Haushofer to construct our own CV of failures. We compiled these with the assistance of our families and friends (in itself a worthwhile exercise, particularly in demonstrating to our children that things don't always work out for us either). Here's a sample of what we came up with:

OUR INVENTORIES OF FAILURE (SO FAR)

Emma:

◊ Failed Year 4 Maths.
◊ Failed to get a part-time job in two department stores at sixteen.
◊ Failed to get into the university course I wanted straight out of school.
◊ Failed the Psychology Statistics unit in first-year university.
◊ Failed the graduate entry exam for the Australian Public Service.
◊ Failed to get interviews for several jobs.
◊ Failed to win several jobs after interview.
◊ Withdrew from Masters Degree.
◊ Failed to be accepted into another degree program as a mature-age student.
◊ Failed to win a number of training contracts and speaking gigs.
◊ Having been accepted as a writer for a magazine, was rejected after the first article I wrote failed to hit the mark.
◊ Failed to sell a single copy of an online program for working parents.
◊ First teen novel rejected four times.
◊ Second teen novel rejected by nine publishers.
◊ Failed to complete five novels.
◊ Came dead last in an 8-kilometre fun run.
◊ Failed to view the Aurora Australis on countless night-time expeditions.
◊ Failed to 'KonMari' the house (or use any other popular decluttering method, for that matter).
◊ First marriage failed.
◊ Failed to breastfeed two of my three children as per 'guidelines'.

◊   Failed to keep my temper with the kids (numerous times).

(The teenagers contributed a screenshot of a Facebook post to add to this list, which read: 'Love me a failed dramatic exit' which apparently pertains to my attempt in 2014 to storm out of the house in disgust at their messy rooms, only to fail in slamming the door properly.)

Audrey:

◊   Failed to make real, lasting friendships in primary school.

◊   Failed to win gold medals in Little Athletics State Championships for my chosen event, race walking.

◊   Failed to hold on to the horse that threw me to the ground at thirteen. Failed to avoid landing in mountains of horse poo. Failed to land without breaking both of my arms.

◊   Failed to select appropriate Year 12 subjects to match my skills and abilities (i.e. choosing Physics, Maths, Biology ... what was I thinking?).

◊   Failed Year 12 matriculation.

◊   Failed to get into a teaching degree at university.

◊   Failed Australian Public Service application process.

◊   Failed to learn how to sew, knit or crochet anything (except sewing on buttons — that I can do).

◊   First marriage failed; failed to recognize any issues in the relationship until it was too late.

◊   Failure to win many client proposals and tender applications for training and coaching work.

◊   Failed to fill several group coaching programs.

◊   Too many cooking failures to mention.

How do we feel, laying out our failures like this for the world to see? Liberated from them. Proud of our persistence and optimism, and our dedication to the pursuit of our goals, despite setbacks. Conscious of a strong desire to give things a go and to stagger up and dust ourselves off when they don't work out.

But honestly? A little part of each of us was tempted to make this an 'annotated' list. We were tempted to include 'what happened next' beside each entry. There was a part of us that felt the need to 'prove' to you that this is only part of our story. But annotating the list would have diluted the point we're trying to make: which is not to hide from failure but to expect it and hurdle over it.

Without embracing the notion of failing, learning, moving on and accepting that everyone around us fails just as much as we do (if not more in the case of those really giving things a red hot go), we can go through life all tangled in thrill-seeking safety gear. We'll avoid going near the edge of the platform. That way, there's no scary whoosh on the way down. There's no holding on for dear life, hoping everything works the way it's supposed to. But there's no bouncing back either. No feeling like you're flying. No sun on your face as you're flung further than you ever imagined you could be.

'COMPARISON-ITIS' IS A CURSE

> Your dreams come crushing down when you tow the wrong path by looking at what others are doing. The Milky Way Galaxy would have been crushed down by now if each planet had left its own orbit to revolve elsewhere!
>
> Israelmore Ayivor

We knew a woman many years ago who seemed to have the fairytale touch of Glinda the Good Witch. On mornings where you'd roll into the school driveway late, your kids polishing off bowls of cereal while they squabbled in the back seat and you hoped no one would notice you weren't wearing a bra, this woman would alight from her stylish vehicle as if it were a five-star salon in which she'd just spent a fortune. She'd usher her pigeon pair of children into the playground, which had been upgraded through her charity efforts as pillar of the school community and President of Everything. There was seemingly no way in which she wasn't winning at life and, as she'd catch your gaze and wave, cheerily, secretly you'd *know*: she wasn't just wearing a bra. She had matching lingerie.

But just occasionally, her defences would be down.

'How do you fit so much in?' you'd ask, admiringly.

'The truth is, I'm so miserably married,' she'd say, 'I have to fill every waking moment.'

If you've ever attended a high-school reunion, or even received an invitation to one, you'll understand that these events tend to elicit feelings of trepidation. It's not just about revisiting a period in time that even the most Enid Blyton-ish ex-student recalls as being punctuated by cringe. It's not only about coming face-to-face with people with whom you may not have chosen to spend your formative years, given a chance. It's not even necessarily about anything that happened at school. It's often about what's happened, and not happened, since.

Organizing a school reunion sheds a whole new light on the secret depths of people's unease. Emails arrive from people apologizing for non-attendance, sparking a deeper chat revealing:

→ 'I haven't done enough.'
→ 'My career is stalled.'
→ 'My marriage has fallen apart.'
→ 'I don't have children.'
→ 'I've put on weight.'
→ 'We're in a mess, financially.'

Comparing yourself to others can be a curse. One of the worst decisions we made not long after we began work on this book was to visit a large bookstore, right in the centre of the city, and check out the other titles in our field. It was about five minutes after we'd sent back the signed publishing contract, when our own book comprised not much more than a bunch of random thoughts scattered across our hotel room wall on coloured sticky notes — many of which were ultimately ditched. Other people's books stood proudly published on the shelves beside each other, with glowing endorsements from famous people and five-star Amazon reviews. The comparison game continued over the coming months while we were neck-deep in a first draft that was full of holes, with paragraphs in the wrong place, repetition and gaps. Others' books seem so beautifully bestseller-worthy. How would our manuscript ever scrape over the line?

It wasn't until we watched a video by US broadcaster Ira Glass on something called 'the taste gap' that we stopped tormenting ourselves. He was talking about creative work, but the advice applies equally to any skill — sport, craft, speaking, project management, baking, teaching — anything where you look at a 'master' in your field and think, 'That's where I'm aiming to be, but I'm falling so far short right now.'

Our lives would stay pretty small if we shrank back every time this 'taste gap' emerged. When we first get a learner's permit to drive a car, we know what good driving looks like. We know we're falling short with all our stalling and swerving and weird parking where we end up way out from the kerb at the wrong angle. At first, the gap can seem insurmountable: how will we *ever* get on the road independently? Yet here most of us are, driving, and we've been doing it successfully for many years now — if not with our eyes shut, certainly while being able to hold conversations or crank up the radio and sing or think about things other than which gear goes where, when.

Sometimes we forget how far we've come. We don't give ourselves enough credit for forging through the 'gap' and finally reaching that, 'By George, I think she's got it!' moment of accomplishment, after which everything becomes easier. And that's because we tend to be our own harshest critics …

IMPOSTER SYNDROME

Emma:

When I was discharged from hospital with my first baby, there was a chunk of me that felt out of place in my own life. Was I really a mother? An actual mother? Like my mother? I found it hard to believe, even as the C-section scar ached under the seat belt during that precarious first drive home. There was a baby asleep in the back seat and apparently we were her parents! I couldn't shake the feeling that we were just playing 'house'.

Then I remember getting a promotion once and thinking, 'Do these people know what they're doing? This is a mistake! I'm not up for this and they'll soon realize it.' The higher the performance ratings, the more amazed I was to have 'scraped through' again. Eventually, I won an Outstanding Service award from the CEO and took this as a sign that proved once and for all that the organization was completely out of touch with reality.

Sometimes, when I travel for business, I think how comical it is that I should be clattering through the airport in a business suit and heels, PowerPoint presentation on the memory stick in my bag, checking emails and coordinating after-school pick-ups like a grown-up.

As a toddler, our young son used to clamber up to the desk at home, bash the keyboard and exclaim proudly that he was 'working!'. Occasionally, I feel the same way — that what I'm passing off as 'work' is really an elaborate game involving a website and masterclasses, published books, articles and corporate clients ... the trappings of the professional world, which is more typically inhabited by people who don't feel like fakes in the airline lounge.

Dr Valerie Young, in her book *The Secret Thoughts of Successful Women: Why capable people suffer from the Impostor Syndrome and how to thrive in spite of it*, describes how the phenomenon of imposter syndrome can hold us back. The thing about 'impostors', she writes, 'is they have unsustainably high standards for everything they do. The thinking here is, "If I don't know everything, then I know nothing. If it's not absolutely perfect, it's woefully deficient. If I'm not operating at the top of my game 24/7, then I'm incompetent."'

We've read the quote above about five times now, trying to convince ourselves that we're not *that* bad, surely, and that we have healthy self-esteem most of the time. And the minute we convince ourselves, we hear, 'Yeah, but ...'. Cue the litany of evidence stacked against us: the times we've fallen, the mistakes we've made, the things we've said to our children in moments of frustration that we desperately wish we could retract, the negative feedback that bucks the trend, and on it goes.

Neuroscientist and TED speaker Bradley Voytek said that, 'Imposter syndrome appears to be fairly rampant among academics and other "smart" people. At some point during your career, possibly more than once, you will look at your peers and think to yourself, "I'm not as good as they are; I am not cut out for this …"'

Audrey:

I was once approached to speak at a conference for senior women in leadership positions within the public sector, about personal effectiveness and team dynamics. I was also asked to deliver a punchy, fast-paced session on content Emma and I created for 'My 15 Minutes' that's similar to some of the topics we've included here.

I received some confirmatory information about the conference, along with a brochure, including details of the other speakers. And that's when the nerves kicked in. Immediately, I started the comparison game. I squared up alongside this impressive list of women and compared myself, unfavourably, to all of them. I seriously began to wonder why the very experienced conference organizers would pick *me* to present to their audience. What could I offer that would add any value, given the calibre of the other presenters? I felt out of my depth.

My old beliefs about not being 'very bright' and never feeling 'clever enough' had been roused from their dormant state to remind me of my limitations. I thought I'd moved beyond the grasp of those beliefs. At least now I was armed with the conscious awareness of these pesky traitors and knowledge of how to overcome them.

So what had brought them back to life? In this case, the answer was glaringly obvious. One of the presenters was a mentor who had set me on my path to professional development over 25 years earlier. Although we work in the same field, I hadn't met her face-to-face in over two decades. And the prospect of that took me right back to being a dorky, 'not bright enough' 21-year-old imposter. Ugh!

I had always seen this woman as someone who had all the answers, as the consummate professional who was experienced, polished and articulate. When we worked together in the early 1990s, she was driven and incredibly savvy, and she represented for me an unattainable benchmark of professional presence and the highest of standards. But she saw something in me at that time, which I certainly hadn't recognized in myself: potential.

The first day of the conference arrived and I was nervous at the prospect of meeting my mentor from all those years ago. Would she see that I had fallen short of expectation in what I'd achieved in the preceding years? Would I lose my ability to have a coherent conversation? She was actually presenting the other full-day workshop of the four-day event, and I assumed she would attend the summit presentations, as I was planning to do. She didn't — and I never saw her. I felt a mix of relief and disappointment. After eliminating the emotional triggers that had dredged up my old limiting beliefs, I realized that deep down I did want to stand up and re-affirm my rightful place on the podium alongside this talented group of female leaders.

Nervously, I waited to be introduced and welcomed to the stage. How ironic that my presentation was all about mindset gremlins that become obstacles to growth, including the hot topics of 'comparison-itis' and imposter syndrome!

I finished the talk on a high. I no longer felt like a fraud. During the break I relaxed and mingled and got to know some of the summit delegates. The feedback from the presentation was excellent. I had tapped into what *New York Times* best-selling author Gay Hendricks would call my 'zone of genius' in his book, *The Big Leap*. There had been a chasm between my pre-session doubts and the reality of my skills and expertise.

In hindsight, the really interesting thing is that no one else was directly involved in the rollercoaster of emotions.

No one had knowingly sabotaged my self-belief. It was all my own doing. As I looked around the room, I wondered if I was the only one.

A belief exists that this form of self-doubt evolved from an outdated survival mechanism, left over from a time when we needed to be permanently on guard. Second-guessing our competence makes us work harder and encourages us to avoid risk and stay safe. Knowing 'what we don't know' isn't a sign of weakness or a red flag to give up — it's a beacon of maturity.

Once we've acknowledged that we're letting feelings of not being 'enough', fear of failure, 'comparison-itis' or imposter syndrome hold us back from a life we want, we can challenge our 'risk-taking' muscle in small ways that, step by step, can begin to overhaul everything.

It's time now for some practical 15-minute experiments, each designed to elevate self-worth and confidence.

INTRODUCING 'MY 15 MINUTES'

It makes sense that the more you have to do, the more important it is to take care of yourself. However, it often seems the more we take on, the faster 'self-care' and personal development slip down the priority scale, until they fall clean off the list. When we're busy with the day-to-day management of career, family and household, the idea of self-improvement can feel about as achievable as finally folding all the washing piled high on the sofa. We know we ought to take better care of our health. We know relationships need energy and work. We know we can take steps towards a career that we love. We know it's possible to have our finances better organized and our house decluttered and still have time for fun and recreation.

We know all of this, but we're wondering *when*?

> When we're snowed under with the small stuff, always playing catch-up, it's easy to slip into 'survival' mode. We sacrifice our own needs and tell ourselves it's only for the next little while, until things calm down.

It's safe to say that if you picked up this book you have a desire to change some things, but you don't currently have long stretches of time available to dedicate to a thorough 'overhaul'. Perhaps you feel stuck, not knowing where to begin, and overwhelmed at the idea of there being so many aspects of your life that you'd love to simplify, change or improve. Maybe you've nodded along at some points in this book that have resonated — and you've realized there are opportunities to step onto a bigger stage, but you're still scared.

That feeling of standing backstage in the wings of change, ready to go on, is tantalizing and terrifying. There's a sense that if you don't go on, you'll feel gutted — and if you do, what will happen?

We've included some powerful and achievable ways to get your act together in seven key areas — health and wellbeing; finances; career and business; home; fun and recreation; relationships; personal growth — in small bursts. Think of these as fun and gentle experiments in taking steps out of your comfort zone towards claiming a more fulfilling life.

Doing the tasks themselves will make a practical difference, but it's just as valuable that you demonstrate to yourself how effective a 15-minute block of time can be. We've given you seven 15-minute challenges at the end of each section in this book, but there are endless ways we can take small steps to improve our lives. Once you move into the 15-minute mindset, you'll realize the power of this 1 per cent of your day.

So, if feeling 'enough' has been a challenge, if courage and confidence have been elusive, if failure has been the enemy … begin with these first seven 15-minute ways to make a difference.

EXPERIMENT 1:
YOUR HEALTH AND WELLBEING
EXCUSE YOURSELF FROM YOUR LIFE FOR A DAY

American author, poet and civil rights activist Maya Angelou said, 'Every person needs to take one day away. Jobs, family, employers, and friends can exist one day without any one of us, and if our egos permit us to confess, they could exist eternally in our absence. Each of us needs to withdraw from the cares which will not withdraw from us.'

The cares which will not withdraw from us …

Sick parents. Sick children. Money worries. Extended family concerns. Sometimes, we can find ourselves so heavily burdened that even our closest families and friends may be unaware of how we're struggling. How on earth would it look if we took time out *now*?

It's up to each of us to take the initiative and 'withdraw ourselves', to step back and away from the drama that will continue to exist in our lives, without there ever being a 'perfect time' to take a break. No matter who or how many people depend on us, we deserve a day away.

Take out your calendar and select a day when you will take the entire day off. Start your 15 minutes by emailing your stakeholders! Boss, partner, kids, babysitter — whoever needs to know — and let them know it's *on*.

Lock in that day and protect it fiercely. This is not a 'tentative' commitment. Be firm and committed, the way you are when other people's priorities are at stake.

Spend the remaining time daydreaming how you'll spend your day off. Remember, this is not a 'catch-up' day for work or washing or wrapping your friends or family in your care. This is a day *away*.

Share your plans for your day away with us on Twitter or Facebook using hashtag #myawayday #idonthavetimebook

EXPERIMENT 2: YOUR RELATIONSHIPS
IT'S THE LITTLE THINGS

Every so often we get sucked into a YouTube vortex of 'grand gestures'. Elaborate marriage proposals, surprise baby announcements, 'gender reveal' parties, 'prom-posals', family reunions, flash mobs … They're heart-warming, tear-jerking and time intensive in a way that takes preparation, organization and many hours of commitment — hours we sometimes say we don't have, despite the hours we've spent in the vortex watching them.

Feel-good gestures don't have to involve an edited video with thousands of 'views'. There are opportunities every day for us to surprise someone with an act of kindness that creates warmth in our world from inside out.

This may, in fact, be a 15-second action, but the consequences will last longer! Choose a way to surprise a person today with a random act of kindness. Here are a few ideas:

* **Pay it forward: buy an extra coffee for the next customer at the café or put a coin in a parking meter.**
* **Leave a book at a bus stop with a note inside for the next person to read it.**
* **Compliment someone to their boss.**
* **Write a thoughtful comment on your friend's blog or social media post.**
* **Send a friend a gift card from an online store.**
* **Bring in the neighbour's rubbish bin.**

EXPERIMENT 3: YOUR CAREER AND BUSINESS FOCUS ON YOUR FABULOUS!

It's one thing lacking confidence when we're beginners and a whole other issue when we doubt ourselves, despite evidence piled up to the contrary, that we're experienced and accomplished at something. If you're feeling out of your depth, it's very likely you are understating your own accomplishments and inflating those of your peers, while you under-emphasize their failures and overstate your own. The result is not an accurate reflection of reality.

Gather and focus on the evidence that, contrary to your inner doubt, you have a solid contribution to make. Dwell on your successes, achievements, positive personality traits and the ability you have to rise above setbacks.

Create what our friend and colleague, Angela Raspass, calls a Fabulous File. This is a box or folder into which you save print-outs of positive feedback, nice emails, expressions of thanks and appreciation, copies of awards, thank-you cards and other examples of your successes that you can browse through any time you need a confidence boost.

* Find a box or folder that suits your purpose.
* Invest 15 minutes to begin the collation of your 'fabulousness'. Be sure to schedule more time in your diary to complete the task later, if necessary, and from now on, print and collect evidence as you go.
* Immerse yourself in the wonderfully genuine feelings of gratitude and appreciation this task will induce.

EXPERIMENT 4: YOUR FINANCES
YOUR WISH LIST

The way we spend money is one of the clearest clues pointing to our values. Spending money on this book, for instance, could be an example of valuing your self-development. Maybe you work in the field of time management or productivity and you've bought this book for your professional library, because you value this topic and your work. Maybe you bought it because you want to spend more time relaxing, looking after your health or more time with your children.

When you look around you at all the things you own (and when you think about the things you have chosen *not* to own) you'll see what matters most to you, and what you value most highly. Maybe it's books and learning, travel and exploration, health and fitness, family, hobbies or house and garden … Everywhere you look, you'll have invested in some areas and sacrificed in others.

The question for this 15-minute challenge is: are you valuing *yourself*?

Imagine you've been handed an envelope addressed to you. Inside is $500. On the outside of the envelope are these instructions: 'This money is for you to spend on yourself. It may not be spent on bills, existing commitments, "needs", donations or gifts to others.'

Take a pen and paper, and write the following:
* A list of reasons why you deserve this gift.
* What would you spend it on? Write your wish list.

EXPERIMENT 5: YOUR PERSONAL GROWTH
FIND YOUR FAILURES

'You may encounter many defeats,' said Maya Angelou, 'but you must not be defeated. In fact, it may be necessary to encounter the defeats, so you can know who you are, what you can rise from, how you can still come out of it.'

Failure takes on many shapes and forms. Sometimes failings are small and inconsequential. Other experiences of failure are life-changing milestones, creating unexpected outcomes. Regardless, accepting — in fact, embracing — failure as a natural occurrence, and one which can bring growth and new opportunities, is essential if we are to reach our true potential.

Earlier, we shared with you some of our failures, and there were many more we didn't include. Now it's time for you to shine a light, albeit briefly, on your failures and look for the humour and lessons, noticing how far you have come.

Spend 15 minutes considering the events, decisions and actions that you would classify as failures in your life. Grab a pen and paper and make a list of these failures. Once you've done this, reflect on how easy or difficult it was for you to create this list. How many of the items were *truly* failures and how many ultimately led to better outcomes for you? Which of them has lessened in potency or seriousness as time has passed?

EXPERIMENT 6: YOUR HOME
TODAY IS SPECIAL

Is your good china in the cupboard? Do you save the best sheets only for visitors? Do you only bring fresh flowers inside when you're hosting a dinner party?

One of the easiest ways that we can enhance our sense of 'home' and 'sanctuary' is by choosing to use the 'best' things. It's also a wonderful way of affirming that we deserve the best in life.

Today, whenever you have a choice between using two different items of the same sort, choose the nicest, most beautiful, most expensive, sentimental or precious one. Use the things you normally save for special occasions.

Treat yourself the way you'd treat an honoured guest in your home. Savour the cup of tea in your finest tea cup, use your most luxurious towels and body-care products. Use the best linen. Bring in fresh flowers at home or work. Buy a gorgeous new mug for your office. Do all of this, even if the rest of your house is a mess or you're staggering under a pile of work at a cluttered desk! Honouring ourselves as more than 'good enough' can start small.

EXPERIMENT 7: YOUR FUN AND RECREATION
CREATE AN UPLIFTING PLAYLIST

We all have certain songs that lift us up and the right music can transform mood, increase energy and help us to create memories of certain events. Music has also been scientifically proven to make you 'smarter', enhance memory and increase learning and retention.

This task is not so much about stepping out of your comfort zone, but rather using music as a tool to evoke strong feelings of confidence and to pump up the feel-good factor. Scientists from the Montreal Neurological Institute and Hospital have found that the pleasurable experience of listening to (or even anticipating) music for 15 minutes releases the feel-good chemical dopamine, a neurotransmitter in the brain important for more tangible pleasures associated with rewards such as food, drugs and sex.

Create your 15-minute playlist — the songs you *know* are going to inspire you into action. (Hint: Start with the songs that never fail to drag you onto the dance floor, even if you're 'not a dancer'.)

The music might become a symbol of the gift you're giving to yourself through taking this 'me time' as you're reading this book (and beyond!). In the future, when you hear this music, it will serve as a prompt to remember that great things can be accomplished in 15-minute bundles. It will help you break down big tasks and remember the 'just do it' mindset.

BEFORE WE MOVE ON ...

'For the most part,' wrote Kristen Hozapfel, author of *Selfless: A social worker's own story of trauma and recovery*, 'I was on the right track to success. I never missed a lecture and my grades were respectable. In the background, however, remained a frisson of doubt.' She continued:

Since entering high school, I'd not been able to shake the feeling that I was missing something my super-smart, long-limbed, pimple-less classmates did not. Of course, logic tells me all those high-school students must have the same pimples, limbs and intelligence of any other regular teenager. Despite this, my heart's memory remains unquestionably clear. I was a lone, pig-tailed human amongst a sea of gorgeous creatures who braided their own hair, effortlessly pulled top marks and knew exactly what to wear on non-uniform days. *How do they know?* I'd wondered.

If only we were granted access to the private thoughts of others, we'd be spared a lot of angst. We'd know that this isn't *Survivor*. Nailing an outfit on non-uniform day in high school isn't being handed the 'Immunity Idol', spiriting away self-doubt. Being handed that big promotion in your forties doesn't make you unflappable. Being 'flappable', even if we hide it well, is part of being human. The secret to risk-taking and progress in the face of potential failure isn't banishing these feelings — it's letting them be without letting them win. 'I'm not ready', 'I'm not good enough', 'I'm happy where I am', 'I'll never be as good as her' are thoughts that are allowed to pass through our mind without us needing to take them and run with them. The way we respond when our mind throws us obstacles informs the way we sculpt our lives.

Thinking you're not up to it, or not good enough, is one of the mindset gremlins that gets its claws into your confidence, but it's not the only gremlin we're tackling. The one we'll cover next is super pesky, a bit of a show-off, and the cause of much of our exhaustion, resentment and overwhelm.

MINDSET GREMLIN 2

WHEN YOU THINK YOU'RE ON YOUR OWN (BUT YOU'RE NOT)

It's time to check in with another set of common beliefs, this time about people-pleasing and being concerned with forming a good impression, or 'doing it all'. This is all about that often well-known sense of feeling overwhelmed by everything that you have to do.

BELIEVE IT OR NOT?

- [ ] I just keep going because everyone is relying on me even though I'm exhausted and need a break.
- [ ] I get really overwhelmed when I have too much on at work and at home, and I don't think I can juggle it all.
- [ ] I can't make time to exercise because it takes time away from the kids.

- [ ] I've got so many things going on, I can't focus on one so I end up doing none.
- [ ] A lot of work needs to be done. I need to clear the existing workload. It never ends.
- [ ] I'm scared of being unable to fit in all my commitments and failing at everything.
- [ ] I have so many things to do, I don't know where to start.
- [ ] I fear telling people 'no' to taking on extra work.
- [ ] I've got information overload: I'm scared of missing the point.
- [ ] I have no time for myself.

A LESSON FROM VANUATU

A young woman we know was volunteering on a remote island of Vanuatu during her gap year, when the country was hit by one of the worst natural disasters in Pacific history. Zoë was on the tiny island of Pentecost when it was battered by the 250 km/hour winds of category 5 Cyclone Pam. The flimsy house where she was staying collapsed. Zoë grabbed the hands of the children she was caring for and bolted with their families downhill towards a different shelter. Trees snapped and fell around them as they ran. At one point she glanced back and thought a large tree had hit a seven-year-old boy who was running behind her. She was sick with fear. But they made it safely to another shelter and hid there until the storm passed.

For the next eight days, Zoë and her island community had dwindling fresh water and food, and no communications. Zoë's parents had no contact with her and no idea whether she was alive, healthy, injured … or worse. All they could do was reach out to the media for help. They were swept into a frenzy of interviews and were in daily contact with the Department of Foreign Affairs and Trade. But it wasn't until over a week later that an Australian Defence Force helicopter flew over the island and spotted Zoë, and her co-volunteer, alive.

The terrain was too rugged to evacuate the teenagers on the spot. The girls were dropped a note and some fresh water and were told to hike for several hours to a clearing the next day.

The phone call Zoë's parents received from that helicopter was, as you'd imagine, the most joyous of their lives. She was safe. She was dehydrated — but she was well.

And she was in tears …

The idea of being singled out for rescue — leaving the villagers Zoë had been living with for months stranded on a devastated island with no food or fresh water — was unpalatable. Zoë had been rescued, but what about them? She begged her parents to help.

They pulled together a fundraising page and shared it with their friends on social media. In just a few days, they'd raised the thousands of dollars needed to buy rice and bottles of fresh water and hire a private helicopter to deliver it. But there was one piece of the puzzle still missing. There was no way to get the supplies from Australia to Vanuatu quickly. Aid was trickling in through the formal agencies, but not fast enough for the villagers on Pentecost Island.

Zoë was distraught. They'd run out of food and fresh water before she'd even been airlifted off the island.

'Why don't we just ask for help?' we suggested. 'Surely someone knows someone … Six degrees of separation and all that?' Fresh from the Harry Styles bandana experience, the obvious course of action seemed to be posting a specific plea on Facebook: 'Does anyone know how to get some food and water from Australia to Pentecost Island in Vanuatu urgently?'

Within minutes, someone responded to the call. A friend's boss had only mentioned *that morning* that he part-owned a coconut oil plantation in Vanuatu. She hadn't known this about him, and when she saw the call for help on Facebook she asked him where the plantation was situated: Pentecost Island. The company shipped there twice a week. And he'd be happy to coordinate the food and water drop from start to finish.

There are times when we feel our request for help is too 'niche'. We convince ourselves that nobody has the time, capacity, resources or interest to assist us. We push on, struggling to do things ourselves — certain we're on our own. But more often than not, it's not that there's nobody available and willing to help us out. It's that we're not prepared to ask.

If a village of starving, dehydrated people can be saved by a random request to deliver very specific items just by asking on Facebook, how much easier might it be to ask for the things we need help with in our daily lives? Someone to pick up the kids because we've got an appointment. Someone to assist with a work deadline. It's not like we're asking for something hard, most of the time. So why don't we just do it?

The excuses of 'I'm on my own' run deep. They're about control, perception and self-esteem. Of all the reasons we overload ourselves and cause our progress to grind to a halt, 'I'm on my own' can have the easiest solution but be the hardest to overcome, because this stuff is often entrenched over many years.

'I'm an independent person!' we'll cry. 'I don't want to inconvenience people. I can handle it myself.' On the surface, these look like admirable qualities, and to a great extent they are. Things fall over, though; time is sucked into unwanted areas of focus and dreams go unrealized if ruthless independence trumps a realistic understanding of our personal limits.

The sky doesn't fall if we don't do everything ourselves. There. We said it.

NOBODY DOES IT AS WELL AS I DO!

You know how it is. There's a report to be written, urgently. You could delegate it to someone on your team. In fact, you *should* delegate it. It's actually their job. You're only meant to sign off on what they put together. But you glance at the calendar. It's due tomorrow. What if they don't write it well enough? What if you have to re-do the work afterwards? It's quite complex. And you'd have to explain what you need, in detail. Wouldn't it just be quicker and easier to write it all yourself?

So you stay back at work and get the thing done. It's *exactly* as you want it. But your email pings. It's another request. This one's for a regular monthly response that should be handed over to a new staff member. It will take you literally 5 minutes to submit the report yourself. Maybe you should just do it this one time and then talk them through the process next month … Surely next month won't be as chaotic? There'll be more time for all this delegation.

Home you go. Your partner's got dinner on. Nice. He's also folded the towels. But, uh-oh! He hasn't folded them *properly*. The towels are folded as rectangles. That's not going to fit neatly in the linen cupboard, is it? *Squares* for the towels! How does he not know this? So you find yourself re-folding them … which is when a child walks out, struggling to thread his arms successfully through a pyjama top. You watch the awkward dressing process for a few seconds and it makes you physically uncomfortable. Without even thinking, you reach out and yank the top over his head and then it's done. The baby is learning to feed herself puréed vegetables. More precisely, she's spraying puréed vegetables across the room like she's at paintball. You can't bear it, whisk the spoon from her hand, wipe her up and feed her yourself. Cleanly.

When 'nobody does it as well as we do', or as quickly, or in our preferred personal style, we can find ourselves bogged down in a whole lot of unnecessary tasks. Things other people could do. Easily. Things other people *have* done, which we re-do, because they haven't done them our way.

Family therapy pioneer Virginia Satir ran a study and found that apparently there are over 250 ways to wash dishes. In every single approach, the dishes came out clean. Yet, every night, in households around the world, there are stealthy dishwasher re-stackers. They open the door, sigh, and completely undo and rearrange another's work. Because nobody else stacks the dishwasher the 'right way'.

When our catch-phrase becomes 'Here! Let me …' it's likely we're over-burdened right now, or will be soon, in every aspect of our lives. We become hoarders of 'all the things'. And we cling on. Hard.

Around us there are people who would love to help. Perfectly capable people. Adults, children. Colleagues, strangers. People rendered helpless by the one-woman, or one-man, multi-act production we're writing, directing, and starring in called, 'I did it my way!'

Lack of delegation wears us out and it frustrates people around us. If we haven't done it already, it won't be long before we throw our hands in the air and scream, 'Everyone's hopeless! No one else bothers! *I have to do everything myself!*'

The good news is we are the architects of this stranglehold that we have on life. We built it, brick by brick, and we can tear it down again and re-build. It doesn't have to be this way.

If you've been hoarding all the responsibility for a long time, the idea of letting go can seem overwhelming at first. It can feel scarily out of control. Letting go — allowing others in — requires trust. It requires a shift in perspective. It needs an acknowledgment that there's more than 'your way' to do things. And we'll give you some experiments on how to begin to undo this on page 84. First, let's look at three other ways you can wind up doing more than you have to, and feeling on your own.

I DON'T KNOW HOW I DO IT

I don't envy 'busy'. Busy means having a schedule, not living life. What I really covet is leisure and peace of mind. Those who have both, have it all.

Donna Lynn Hope

Jane worked in a senior role in a large advertising agency. She stayed back most nights, which meant she could go straight from work to slash through her super-human schedule of evening committees and appointments. No matter how much she had on, she could always fit more in — to the astonishment of people around her.

One day her boss sent an email to a group of staff at Jane's level, asking each of them to contribute one section for her boss's report. Jane hit 'reply all' and told everyone to stand down on the request. She'd write the entire report. And she'd do this despite already being overburdened, overcommitted and on the edge of burning out.

We asked Jane why she'd done this.

'It's the praise I get when I do this stuff. People don't know how I fit so much more in and that feels good.'

The benefits were short-lived. Her fiancé was getting annoyed. They'd been engaged for a while but hadn't found time to plan the wedding. Jane could hear the biological clock ticking and was beginning to wonder how she'd squeeze a baby into her life. The only time she could schedule a conversation about this was in the car, in peak-hour traffic, between two after-work appointments.

When we cram things into our schedules because of a belief that being busy equals being significant, we're being 'badge of honour' busy. Keeping our schedules at least as jam-packed (if not more) as the schedules of the people around us keeps us at least as important as everyone else, if not more important … at least in our minds. It's one way for us to create our worth.

People say, 'I don't know how you do it!' and the truth is, you don't know how you do it either — or even if you want to. All you know is that other people notice and admire how much you're doing. And that feels good. What doesn't feel good is the chaos this causes in our lives. The exhaustion. The pushing of our own interests off our priority lists. It doesn't feel good to notice our friends having down-time and relaxing on weekends, while we're coaching the game, typing up the meeting minutes, studying for a course we're not enjoying and doing the endless taxiing for our kids, our kids' friends and our kids' friends' friends …

It reaches a point where the pay-off in admiration isn't worth the secret resentment. You're sick of being busy just for the sake of looking important and feeling worthwhile. You're sick of trying to be noticed. Sick of the endless one-upping, personal-besting and investment of time you'd much rather spend on something else, thrown into what amounts to the creation of a professional and personal CV that to everyone else looks 'wow' but to you feels more than a bit 'meh'.

But how can you let this go? What happens if you quit the extra commitments? What if you work just regular hours and not overtime? What happens if the odd weekend is reduced to pottering around at home, reading the newspapers over a long lunch and going to the movies? Galloping FOMO — fear of missing out — is giving you palpitations. *What will people think?*

'Badge of honour' busy is a descendant of the fear that we're not enough as we are. We want people to notice us and admire the way we handle things. We want to impress people with the sheer volume of things we take on and get through (not that we'd ever admit it in so many words) — but, behind it all, the busyness doesn't plug the hole. It's a facade. It's all for show. It's an attempt to compete and keep up and measure up against people who, in the main, are not aware they're even in the race, and it's *exhausting*.

Awareness that this is happening is the first step towards untangling ourselves from it. The mindset tweak to look for here is a switch from *craving* significance to 'giving' it. Think of it as standing behind the spotlight and directing its beam, instead of darting around chasing the light. Switch your focus, so you start to think about who you can help or build up, not for your own gratification but for theirs.

When you're no longer running ragged chasing significance from others, a remarkable shift occurs. The world itself seems more significant. Your place in the world becomes more obvious and secure. You become more comfortable in your own skin, and your time opens up.

And if the Badge of Honour Gremlin is a time thief, its partner in crime is surely the adorable, affable, helpful, charming and wonderful, worn-out and secretly resentful gremlin friend who can't say 'no'.

GETTING APPROVAL

We may call it 'people pleasing', but it is entirely self-serving because it is really all about keeping myself comfortable. Boiled down, it could be more accurately called 'me pleasing'.

Emily P. Freeman,
Grace for the Good Girl: Letting go of the try-hard life

Audrey:

I found a series of emails recently, sent 18 days after my second son, Will, was born. 'Let me know if there's anything I need to help with on the new project,' I offered in one email (as if the drugs from the C-section hadn't yet worn off). 'At least, anything to do from home ... I won't be driving for a week or two yet.' I went on to explain that my son was 'still having trouble working out that night time is for sleeping ...' (which at 18 days old seems perfectly reasonable, in hindsight!) 'and we're all unwell right now, but doing fine.'

A couple of weeks later, while still on leave, I found myself accepting some unplanned work, which meant that I sat at my computer all day, 5-week-old baby snoozing on a feeding pillow on my lap, stopping only to feed and change him when he needed it (and not to feed myself or go to the toilet), in order to meet the deadline.

Why?

Because I was asked. And I didn't want to let someone down.

A few years later, I still hadn't learned. Most Friday nights my family and I get together with our neighbours out on the front deck of one of their houses. It's something we all look forward to — sharing the highlights and lowlights of our weeks, with a glass of wine, some snacks and sometimes a shared, casual dinner. On hot nights, we sometimes head into our back garden for impromptu pool parties and meals cobbled from whatever we have in the fridge and pantry.

It's the easy, casual nature of these nights that I love. I avoid booking other commitments on a Friday night just in case we wander across the road with a glass in hand for a chat. We've been doing this for a number of years now and it's been lovely to see our kids grow to look forward to Friday Night Fun with their friends from the street — some of whom they've known all their lives. They play, they dance, they make up games and entertain us with their talent shows, they chase each other in the darkness and they cover entire driveways with chalk drawings.

When our son, Finlay, was about 5 years old, he came with me into the office of his school one Friday morning, while I spoke to a staff member. There were a number of other administration and teaching staff chatting behind the reception desk while my query was being handled. One of them asked Fin whether he was going to the school disco that evening. He looked up at me briefly with his big blue eyes before looking back at the woman.

'No. Mummy didn't buy me a ticket because she and Daddy will be going out drinking with the neighbours tonight … as usual.'

What. Just. Happened.

I was *mortified*! My heart sank — my face burning red with embarrassment. What kind of mother *am* I? Worse — what kind of mother do *they* think I am?

In that moment I had two choices. I could explain to them about our very family-friendly Friday Night Fun gatherings and clarify that we're not irresponsible lushes who abandon their children on a quest to party the night away. Or I could look at my innocent child, chuckle at his deadpan humour, buy a ticket for the disco he didn't want to attend and declare, 'Oh yes, of course! Thanks for reminding me. I knew there was something else I needed to do when I popped in here this morning.'

I'm sorry to report I chose option two. I lied. I took the easy way out — or rather the option which was less embarrassing for me at the time.

Sometimes we make choices we'd rather not make because we imagine what other people will think of us if we say no. We save face. We seek favour. We cave in. But at what cost to us?

Clearly, in this situation the 'cost' to me was minimal — I traded a relaxing Friday night at home for a couple of hours of 100-plus kids running riot in a school gym. It was worth it, too, to see the unrestrained and unabashed glee on my son's face as he got over his fears and danced wildly to Michael Jackson and ABBA songs, like only a 5-year-old can.

I traded my mortification for initial disappointment and it all worked out well in the end. No big deal. At least not that time. But when you find yourself caving regularly to others' expectations (or what you perceive those expectations to be) in little ways like this, or in much bigger ways, life starts looking a lot less like the shape you desire, and a lot more like the shape other people desire for you.

It usually starts in early childhood: the realization that people love it when you do nice things for them, when you help them out or say 'yes' when asked. Your actions are reinforced. You're told you're a 'good kid'. You learn that you're 'reliable' and 'conscientious'. It feels good that people trust you and ask you to help. It feels great to have their approval.

Getting approval is like a drug. You crave it, but in order to feel its benefits you need increasing amounts. You have to do more. And the more you take on and do, the more you're asked. Next thing, you're the busy person after whom they named 'Ask A Busy Person' syndrome and conversations are happening like these:

'Can you help out at the school?'

No, you think. *I've got that project due for work and I'm already behind.* What comes out of your mouth, though, is, 'Sure! What time do you need me?'

'Are you able to pick up the teenagers from the party on Friday night?'

Actually, that's the night we were going to have a date for the first time in over a month, since my husband's been away for work. 'Of course! What's the address?'

'If someone doesn't volunteer to coach the under sixes, we're going to have to cancel the season.'

I have to move my parents into a nursing home this month, and I don't even like soccer. 'Sure. Will I bring the oranges too?'

Maybe your examples aren't as extreme as these, or maybe they're worse. If you can't say 'no' and your schedule is crammed with things you don't want to do, you could be suffering what author Jacqui Marson calls 'The Curse of Lovely'. It becomes harder and harder to say 'no' because you don't want to shatter the reputation you've built for being helpful and kind, reliable, dependable and 'always there' for people.

To help manage the people-pleasing problem better, Texan professor and best-selling author Brené Brown bought herself what she calls a 'boundary ring'. It's a silver ring that she spins 'during those awkward moments when an ask hangs in the air'. While she spins it, she silently repeats her boundary mantra: 'Choose discomfort over resentment.' This reminds her to stop and think before delivering what used to be an automatic 'yes'.

Delivering the 'no' need not be accompanied by a complex monologue of excuses. 'I can't help you this time, but thanks for asking. I hope it goes well,' is enough. Those moments where we say, 'I'm sorry, I can't' or 'No, I'm not available' do feel uncomfortable (excruciatingly so, if you're not used to it), but it's so much easier to feel uncomfortable for a few moments than it is to feel resentful for much longer when you take on more and more tasks that spill all over your diary and overcomplicate your life.

It's not easy to be a recovering people-pleaser, but it's definitely worth it. You might look all sunshine and endless activity and thoughtfulness on the outside, but inside you're quietly drowning. Or seething. Or both. You *know* the oxygen mask has to be fitted to yourself first. You get that you can't go on like this indefinitely. Your struggle is wanting to turn this ship around without offending someone. As Jacqui Marson explains, it's about learning to be 'lovely, with choice'. It's about being compassionate, with boundaries. It's about having courage to believe you are still going to be regarded as a kind, likeable person — even if, from time to time, you make some decisions that some people don't like.

There's being 'badge of honour' busy. There's struggling to say 'no' through a need to be liked. And then there's being a fully-fledged, dyed-in-the-wool, burn-me-at-the-stake, martyr …

MARTYR SYNDROME

My grandmother always acted in other people's interests, whether they wanted her to or not. If they'd had an Olympics in martyrdom my grandmother would have lost on purpose.

Emily Levine

'My manager is driving us all mad!' a friend confided. 'She is *such* a martyr! Takes work home unnecessarily every night and on weekends and talks about it the next day. She had a headache the other day during a meeting and refused to take a 2-minute break for some pain relief, even though everyone urged her to stop. Someone got up in the end and found two tablets, along with a glass of water — and even then she only took one. Because it looks so much better to be pushing through with a headache, doesn't it!'

If we act like a martyr we're operating under the mistaken belief that the buck stops with us. It might feel like that's the case, but it almost always isn't. There are plenty of people who would help us out if asked: a neighbour, colleague or friend, a family member, an acquaintance, a stranger or a charity group.

Sometimes pride causes us to act like a martyr, or a genuine fear of putting people out, a fear that 'everyone else has their own stuff to deal with, so I can't add to it'. Most often, though, when there's a sense that we are *always* the one left doing everything, it's martyrdom.

Struggling through, pushing on, refusing help, doing it all yourself … being a martyr is hard work! Doing it tough becomes the vehicle to being noticed. It's how you keep afloat and ahead. You can't do 'self-care' or take time off, or book a holiday, or relax. How would that look? Lazy? Worse — you might sink into the crowd …

Doing more than necessary and making everything harder than it needs to be isn't the kind of epitaph martyrs aim for, but it's how they're remembered. Friends and family can unwillingly be pushed aside in the process of martyrdom, and rendered redundant. There's nothing 'equitable' about a friendship or relationship with a martyr. There can't be, because the martyr feels threatened if they're not busier and more tired than everyone else.

In families, this plays out with one person taking responsibility for everything. It's usually under the guise that, 'my partner just won't think' or 'the kids don't pull their weight'. In reality, it's that the martyr won't allow others competence and contribution because that moves everyone onto a dangerously equal footing. A footing where the martyr doesn't feel special any more.

Like people who strive to be 'badge of honour' busy, martyrs have a strong need for significance. Unlike the 'badge of honour' brigade, however, who derive significance from the wow factor, martyrs tend to seek this through empathy: 'You poor thing, having so much to do!'

We're not on our own, even when we think we are. There's no need for us to have as much to do as we sometimes like to demonstrate. There's a pile of available ways to fill our time, and a whole lot of choice that we're ignoring that could radically transform how we feel about our lives, if we spent our time in more enjoyable and productive ways. Let's tackle this sense of wanting to do it all with some 15-minute experiments in letting go, letting others in and making space to enjoy ourselves.

EXPERIMENT 8:
YOUR HEALTH AND WELLBEING
ASK FOR HELP

Asking for help is a sign of courage. Vulnerability is indicative of strength. Allowing someone to see us not at our best but at our most vulnerable, is a gift. Everyone needs help at some stage or another. Being able to recognize and be comfortable with the fact that no one is able to do it all, all the time, is a sign of really having embraced the meaning of 'community'.

This task is about creating a wellbeing wish list.

If you could ask for help with anything at all, what would it be and who might you ask? Write down fifteen things that others could do for you, taking no more than 1 minute for each item on your list. (No overthinking! Write down anything that comes to mind.) It may be outsourcing something, it could be asking a neighbour or fellow school parent to bring your kids home from school, it might be seeking advice on an issue you're struggling with privately.

EXPERIMENT 9: YOUR RELATIONSHIPS
HEARTFELT THANKS

When Emma's elder daughter was fifteen, she encouraged everyone on her school bus to sign a thank-you card for the driver at the end of the year. She and a friend delivered a 'speech' on the last day of school about how grateful they were that he'd put up with their loud singing of One Direction songs, and screaming and squealing, and had greeted them all by name every day all year. The driver cried and explained that they had no idea what this meant to him. He spoke to the school principal and his boss about it. It genuinely moved him.

The girls' gesture inspired us to incorporate a 'thank-you' task into our program. People in our program use this opportunity to express gratitude for all kinds of purposes — to mend fences, speak their hearts or track people down with whom they'd long lost contact. The results, at best, bring love back. At a minimum, they bring peace knowing they had said what needed to be said.

Think of someone who has made a difference in your life, whether they're someone you love deeply, someone who did something life-changing or life-saving for you — or even the person on the checkout at the supermarket who is cheerful each week despite long, cranky, peak-hour queues filled with people rolling their eyes about the lack of staff. Write, call, email, contact their manager, send flowers — however you wish to express your gratitude, just do it. Then watch as some magic transpires.

EXPERIMENT 10:
YOUR CAREER AND BUSINESS
IT'S YOUR CHOICE

When we say 'no' we give meaning to our 'yes'. Until we're clear on what our 'yes' is, we'll find that we allow our diaries to fill up with things that aren't meaningful to us.

The first step in moving from approval-seeking towards 'compassion with boundaries' is to work out what matters most to us. You need to know which things are 'golden' to you — those things (people, activities, time) that are most precious and worthy of your protection. It's up to each of us to make clear our own boundaries. This requires being clear on what we can take on, changing our situation if we have taken on too much (by negotiating and delegating, postponing and cancelling) and learning to be more aware, earlier on, of exactly how much we can handle reasonably.

First, consider in just a few words the 'big picture' legacy you wish to leave. When you look back at the end of your life on your contribution to the people around you personally and professionally — and to the wider community and the world — what do you want to be able to say that you did? Write it down. (This is a 15-minute task, so you're going for some broad ideas here, not an intricate, word-perfect plan.)

Now look at your calendar or diary and ask whether the choices you're making now are going to allow you to leave that kind of legacy. Is all the running around that you're doing for others moving you towards leaving the legacy that means a lot to you, or further away from it? If some change is needed, begin with small shifts in your boundaries. It's almost certainly possible to extricate yourself from some of the things to which you're already committed, though it's easier to start from now and shape things differently with future requests. Look for opportunities to say no and give meaning to your 'yes'. Find and act upon:

* something you can cancel
* something you can postpone
* something you can delegate.

EXPERIMENT 11: YOUR FINANCES
BE PROACTIVE

The topic of finances can bring up a range of feelings for different people, from a deep sense of abundance and security in some, to gut-wrenching anxiety and fear in others. When coupled with a feeling of being 'on my own with this', financial worry can lead us to believe that the situation is actually more dire than it might be. Sometimes this is because we aren't sharing this struggle with a partner, or it might be because they don't *appear* willing to get involved and help work through the issues. And sometimes we are simply too concerned to really dig deeper and look for solutions. We hope it will all magically disappear. We opt for shame and avoidance.

According to financial coach Sylvia Chierchia, financial stress can consume all areas of your life and how you deal with it can affect the relationships with your partner, children, friends, and even your employer or your clients. She says, 'Many people blame the outside world when it comes to money management. Whilst things like the economy and high cost of living are valid factors, it can often just be our beliefs and the underlying meaning that we have placed on money and wealth that can be a major component to the financial stress we feel in our lives.' Chierchia highlights the importance of identifying where the cause for financial stress lies so you can isolate the steps you'll need to take in order to deal with that stress.

Regardless of the state of your finances, seeking help, support and advice is essential to creating long-term financial security. Being proactive can make all the difference. The good news is that if you are at all feeling the burden of financial stress, you don't need to face it alone. Invest 5 minutes now to assess your financial health. Look through your records and get a ballpark

estimate of your current financial status, including your readily accessible cash, your short- to mid-term investments and your retirement investments (superannuation or private pension funds). Also take into account your short- and long-term liabilities.

Then use the next 10 minutes to do one of the following:

* If you have a partner, agree on a time to sit down and work through your finances together. Your aim will be to create a budget, agree on responsibilities, such as who will pay the bills, and share the load.
* If you already have a financial adviser, book an appointment with them or with an accountant to discuss any issues which are concerning you.
* If you don't have an adviser, start researching to find a reputable one. Ask people you trust for recommendations — friends, family, colleagues and your bank.
* Also consider hiring a financial coach — they can help eradicate the underlying limiting beliefs that often lead to financially stressful situations.
* If you do not have a current will, make an appointment with a solicitor and make one.

EXPERIMENT 12: YOUR PERSONAL GROWTH
BE YOUR OWN BEST FRIEND

No matter how close we are to our dearest friends and family members, and how open we are with others in general, we each tend to keep a part of ourselves hidden from the rest of the world. It's that secret knowledge that we hold about who we are, or what we think, or fear, or what we're doing (or have done). It's the kind of thing that we might dwell on at 3 a.m. and be afraid to share — even with those we trust the most.

Take 15 minutes to think about something you hold closest and most private, perhaps something you've been tormenting yourself about.

Imagine that you are your own best friend, and tell yourself what you need to hear. Deliver it the way you'd speak to your best friend: with love, compassion, forgiveness, kindness and tact — while being absolutely frank. Find time to say it aloud if you can, or to write it down.

15 MINUTE MAGIC

Remember, it is very likely that you are your own harshest critic. Learning to be kind to ourselves is a life skill that takes practice and patience.

EXPERIMENT 13: YOUR HOME
LET IT GO

Building a team to share the load opens a gold mine of extra time. Learning to stand back while others develop competence might, at first, be challenging if you're used to doing it all yourself, but it's worth it.

Start with one small thing. It could be loading the dishwasher or folding the towels. Maybe it's letting a child select the day's outfit or letting go of an element of a project at work. Pick one thing, take a breath, and let someone else step up. And while that's happening, start to think about how you'd fill the time you could free up by getting better at letting go and delegating.

All those things you've been saying you 'don't have time' to do ... what are they? Spend some time considering how different your life might look if you prioritized them.

EXPERIMENT 14: YOUR FUN AND RECREATION PLAYTIME

You've worked hard to scramble to first place in the 'to do list' stakes. But learning to let other people shine — building people up — is an amazing gift, and it's one that keeps on giving! The more you allow others to step up, the more you get to step back — and the more time you liberate for more important things.

With responsibility sometimes comes a reduction in the amount of fun we can squeeze into our schedules as adults. However, playfulness is key to creativity and to wellbeing, and can greatly improve relationships. When we 'play', we temporarily switch off from our more 'grown-up' concerns, and our downtime is often when inspiration and creativity strike.

Write a list of the activities you used to do for fun, when your life was less encumbered than it is today. Think of how you spent your time, who you hung out with, what you did, whether you exercised or played sport, played a musical instrument, whether you took creative classes, what you read or watched and how you relaxed.

Now pick one activity from your list — the one which really makes you smile when you remember it — and schedule a time in the near future to reconnect with it, even for old time's sake. It could mean watching one of your favourite movies, going ice skating, having a night out dancing or relaxing with a picnic rug and a book at a place that brings back great memories.

At first, these might seem to be 'indulgent' and rather 'inglorious' ways to fill your spare time — remember, though, the purpose here isn't to earn points or attention, it's not to impress anyone: it's just to enjoy.

BEFORE WE MOVE ON ...

Sometimes the line between chasing your own dreams and doing the right thing by the people around you can seem blurry. When we interviewed Julie Godwin, winner of the Australian TV show *MasterChef*, she explained that she'd been allowed out of the 'compound' the TV contestants had been staying in, for Mother's Day. 'At 1 a.m. with my shoes in one hand and my bag in another, I was sneaking out of the house like a naughty teenager,' she explained. She had a wonderful night at home, but it was over too fast. 'Back at the compound, I said to my husband, "I don't think I can do this. I want to go home. Please take me home." And my husband said to me, "Put your game face on, babe. Go back in there and finish what you started. Stay there, but win the bloody thing!"'

'If I'd quit,' Julie explained, 'I don't think I would ever have quite forgiven myself. We would have spent the rest of our lives wondering "What if?"' Since winning *MasterChef*, Julie has released three cookbooks, regularly appears on other TV shows, has opened her own cooking school and now co-hosts a breakfast radio show. Her candid interview reminded us that behind every successful person is a *story*. Things are never as straightforward as they appear on the surface. We don't know what happens behind closed doors or when the cameras are off — even (or perhaps especially) on 'reality' TV.

Solutions are never packaged up perfectly for us, and there must be give and take. Julie's decision to continue the competition was tough on her and on her family at the time, but inevitably changed all of their lives in exciting ways. 'If you want something enough and if you have persistence and determination, you can achieve it,' she advised. 'Unwrapping myself from that embrace and walking back through that door is one of the hardest things I've ever done. A different decision could have changed everything.'

We're not on our own and we don't have to do everything ourselves, even when it feels like it. We exist within a thriving social ecosystem where we are available to help other people, and others are available to help us. It takes a village not just to raise children, but to run the full gauntlet of adult life. If we don't have help, it's often because we've studiously avoided it. We haven't invited help in, even when it's been offered. We've often made excuses that 'we're on our own with this' because:

→ we're clinging to control, thinking 'nobody does it as well as I do'
→ being 'badge of honour' busy gives us a sense of worth
→ we're suffering the 'Curse of Lovely' as people-pleasers
→ we're shutting help out because the empathy we receive as martyrs feels good.

There's so much to gain by letting this stuff go — not just better health and wellbeing, and more time to do what matters most to each of us, but deeper and more genuine relationships. Admitting we can't do it all and asking for help is an exercise in vulnerability, in taking off the covers and showing up as we truly are, despite our fear of rejection. It's is a sign of strength. Some of the most confident and capable people we know have embraced the idea that they can't do it all. It's why Oscar acceptance speeches are so long. Successful people have so many people to thank for helping them get there!

Any activity that shuts people out, or causes imbalance in a relationship — and anything we take on because it makes us look better or busier, or helps us wrangle the 'What will people think?' demon — is going to reduce our quality of life. It might feel good for a while, to be buzzing on the high of people-pleasing or doing more than everyone else — but this is a short-lived, 'sugary' high that is inevitably followed by a crash. That crash looks a lot like private resentment, secret comparison and an empty feeling that, no matter how hard you try to impress people, it's never going to be enough.

The moment you choose to let go and start getting through the world *with* people, instead of *in competition* with them, is the moment all of this self-inflicted pressure starts to ease. It's the moment you get your life back. Because, somewhere out there, probably only a social media click away, is someone who's prepared to help you move a shipment of life-saving goods to some stranded villagers in a foreign country. Or they're ready to bake your family a lasagne because they know you're not well. Or they're happy to write a paragraph for your boss's report so you don't have to do it all. They're ready to give you a lift, or help you fix the side fence or lend you a cup of sugar, or an ear, or a shoulder to lean on or some money to pay your heating bill.

Most people don't do such favours because they feel sorry for you, or because they want you to owe them. They're just decent human beings, prepared to roll up their sleeves and help you get through. When you're prepared to do the same for them, it's not about dependence or independence. It's about interdependence, which is the foundation of our deepest and most rewarding relationships and life experiences.

So far, we've wrangled the mindset gremlins of 'not good enough' and 'I have to go it alone'. Another way that we thieve our own time involves squandering it in the unproductive activities of overwhelm, perfectionism and procrastination. That's what we're going to move on to next.

MINDSET GREMLIN 3

WHEN YOU THINK YOU'VE GOT TO GET IT RIGHT (BUT YOU DON'T)

Perfectionism and procrastination can bring us to a standstill. How many of these beliefs resonate with you?

BELIEVE IT OR NOT?

- ☐ If my work isn't 100 per cent correct it isn't good enough.
- ☐ I always worry I don't have the skills I need to do a good job.
- ☐ I worry my decisions are not the right ones.
- ☐ What if what I do is not good enough, or does not meet expectations?
- ☐ I can't do 'all' my work because quality will drop.
- ☐ People will see me fail or be imperfect. I only do something if I know I can do 100 per cent.

- [ ] There's no point trying unless I'm guaranteed to succeed.
- [ ] When I'm doing a project that I'm really excited about, I procrastinate by chasing irrelevant tangents related to the task. I'm 'doing' the task but not effectively.
- [ ] I don't know where to begin and how to begin.
- [ ] I procrastinate using other work (e.g. not doing high priority items and justifying it by doing easier, less important tasks).

A LESSON FROM NEW YORK

One of our greatest learnings came after speaking to a group of bankers in a high-rise building in Sydney, with gorgeous views of the harbour. The seminar was about a range of productivity topics, including how it feels to be ludicrously overwhelmed by too much to do.

One of the managers shared probably the most powerful story we'd ever heard, on the topic of 'overwhelm'. He spoke about his experience working in New York after September 11, when he was given the grisly task of rebuilding the branch of the business that had been located in one of the Twin Towers. There was no physical office space, no furniture or technological equipment, no records and files. Worse, he had to recruit an entire office of staff into positions previously occupied by people he admired, respected and loved.

Imagining the intensity of what he faced, suddenly every work-related hurdle that we'd ever encountered seemed to pale in significance: the times we'd battled several competing tasks, struggled with a difficult colleague or been forced to step up and take something over in someone's absence. Those experiences had seemed challenging enough for us, but it was incredibly humbling listening to someone who was handed the kind of once-in-a-lifetime pressure we hope we'll never encounter — starting from scratch amidst the physical, personal and emotional ruins of that terrorist act.

The manager explained that he'd felt completely overwhelmed both professionally and personally. He was 'staring at a brick wall which towered over me and cast me in pitch dark, obscuring any clue on where to begin'. He turned to his mentor, who agreed that yes, there was an imposing brick wall. What he had to do was to reach out and remove just one brick — it didn't matter which one — and doing so would let in a shard of light. That light would be enough to illuminate the next brick, and then the next ... So, from the rubble of his own Ground Zero, this manager reached out and removed that first brick. As more and more light flooded through the small gap that he created in the wall, he began to see what he had to do. He was able to pick up speed and move with purpose. With this 'just one brick' strategy, he led his shattered team out of the darkness, at a time when they needed him most.

The application of the 'one brick' strategy at times when we can't see where to begin — 'triaging' tasks not by urgency or priority, but randomly until there's enough light to make decisions — has changed the way we cope with the professional and personal demands in our lives. At times of real overwhelm, getting our priorities right can be beyond us. It's not about doing the right things first, it's about doing *anything*, and getting ourselves unstuck.

Let's look now at situations where our progress is held back and our time eaten up because we're 'doing' overwhelm. And be clear, overwhelm is a doing word! Making hot drinks, tidying your desk, emailing friends to complain about how overburdened you are ... this isn't being overwhelmed, it's 'doing' overwhelm. And when you're a master at overwhelm, there are so many brilliant ways to stunt your progress.

IT HAS TO BE PERFECT

When one of our friends first dreamt up her 'big idea' for a business she went into full-blown planning mode. She showed us the gorgeously colour-coded binders she'd organized in her office, the perfectly chosen colours and fonts in her branding, the stunning website still under construction after many months. She developed materials, templates, client correspondence, filing systems ... She was good to go!

But the problem was she wasn't going. She was stuck in an endless cycle of 'duck lining-uppery'. Nothing could shake her out of this state of constant preparation until, late one night, she was watching a television interview on one of the more intellectually rigorous current affairs programs, on her topic of speciality, delivered by a competitor in her field, who, while arguably less qualified and knowledgeable than her, had the advantage of actually being 'out there' and getting on with it. That was the moment for her. No more mucking around and obsessively chasing perfection. No more, 'I just need to set this bit up, or spruce up that bit, then I'll be ready.' It was time to leap.

A couple of years later, we caught up with our friend after she herself had been interviewed on national television. She'd been given almost no warning about the appearance and very little time to prepare. To her surprise and delight, the interview flowed beautifully. She was on top of her game. She recalled what she needed to recall, expressed it articulately and came away with a buoyant sense that she really knew her stuff. Compared with previous media appearances, her performance in this interview was a cut above the rest. It was also more enjoyable.

The difference? She hadn't over-prepared. She wasn't trying too hard, because there wasn't enough time for that. She relied on the knowledge she had and took heart in the idea that it would all rise to the surface on cue. It had to! Since then she's appeared on television many times. Her career and her business have skyrocketed. She received a publishing deal based on the work she was doing and now *she* is known as the expert in her field. She's the expert because she's not trying to be perfect any more.

PERFECTION IS A TRAP

British psychologist Richard Wiseman conducted a 10-year study on luck. He followed 400 participants, some of whom considered themselves very lucky in life, love and career, and others who considered themselves unlucky.

In personality tests, the 'unlucky' group were found to be more tense and routine-driven. Anxiety disrupts people's ability to notice the unexpected — a crucial factor in creating or seizing chance opportunities. To test this, Wiseman gave each participant a copy of a newspaper and asked them to count the number of photographs it contained. On page two there was a half-page advertisement that said, in bold type, 'STOP COUNTING. THERE ARE 43 PHOTOGRAPHS IN THIS NEWSPAPER.' Wiseman found that those who had pre-identified as 'lucky' were more likely to notice this ad. They expected good things to happen.

People miss out on wonderful opportunities when they are too focused on looking for something specific. They go to parties intent on finding their perfect partner, and miss opportunities to find new friends. They do an internet search for the perfect job, discounting other jobs.

In Wiseman's experiments, those who were trying harder performed below those who were more relaxed and open and 'went with the flow' without an expectation of 'doing it perfectly'. People who were more relaxed were also found to be more 'lucky'. It's similar to those times when you're trying, unsuccessfully, to think of a word, or someone's name, or a book title, and it comes to you effortlessly, later, when you're not trying. The brain functions best with a break.

A combination of adequate preparation and relaxation works best. How do you do that? How do you switch off? Nature loves a vacuum, so if you stop preparing and launch straight into doing 'nothing', you're likely to drift back into preparation mode unless you can fill that void with something else.

Switching 'channels' gives your subconscious mind time to do its stuff. Because it's that part of the brain — the part that's whirring away all the time beneath our rational thinking — that you can count on during unexpected media appearances, or while struggling to think of a word, or when you're suddenly on show, unprepared according to your own high standards, and having to get on with it anyway.

I JUST NEED TO DO THIS FIRST

> The habit of always putting off an experience until you can afford it, or until the time is right, or until you know how to do it is one of the greatest burglars of joy. Be deliberate, but once you've made up your mind — jump in.
>
> Charles R. Swindoll

Thirty-six thousand words into writing this book, we hit a snag. Ironically, the snag was this page, and this chapter, about procrastination. We hadn't found a story powerful enough to illustrate the point we wanted to make, so we highlighted this bit in red in the manuscript and decided to come back to it the next day.

At the end of the next day, and all across the following week, the font stayed red. We still felt stuck and it seemed too hard, so we abandoned fixing this chapter and tinkered around with the bits we'd already done instead. They were prettier. We could move words around decoratively and play with sentences that were already there, pretending it was a worthwhile use of our time.

Then *boom!* A fabled story leapt out at us from the internet and it was perfect! The 'Seinfeld Strategy' of productivity was related by Brad Isaac, a young comedian who reportedly asked Jerry Seinfeld for any 'tips for a young comic' one night when they bumped into each other backstage at a gig. Seinfeld told Isaac that coming up with better jokes was the way to become a better comic, and the way to do that was to write every day. He suggested that the young comic mark a wall calendar with a large cross each day he wrote, with the increasing number of crosses forming a growing chain once he got into the habit of writing more and more often.

What's great about this example is that it doesn't matter if you're not in the mood. It doesn't matter about the quality of your work. All that matters is not breaking the chain, doing what you said you'd do, every day.

What wasn't great about this example was that it turns out Jerry Seinfeld never said it. Worse, he is quoted on Reddit as saying, 'This is hilarious to me, that somehow I am getting the credit for marking an X on a calendar with the Seinfeld Productivity Program.' The irony is that discovering the bogus non-Seinfeld productivity strategy and starting to write about it was all we needed to get over our writer's block, stop procrastinating and steer this show back on the road. It stopped us from polishing the bits we'd already written, kidding ourselves that what we were doing was 'progress'.

Remember in primary school when you'd begin a new unit of work by creating a fancy title page? The page looked good but it didn't teach you anything or move you forward. It was just a precursor to the 'real work' that was to come. 'Colouring in the title page' might feel like work but it's really just another way to procrastinate. Unless you are a graphic designer and you are actually creating a title page, move on, because that kind of 'work' is rarely done in the name of progress but at the expense of it. We don't jump in because we're scared, or unsure, or feel more confident at the stage we're at. We're worried we'll make a mess of it. It's easier to stay 'clean' where we are, instead of wading around in the muck of uncertainty.

In our case, it was writing. In yours, maybe it's reading articles about cold calling instead of cold calling. Or it's being overly choosy about the layout of your business cards instead of meeting with potential clients. Maybe it's having unnecessary planning meetings instead of working on the project. It *feels* like you're working but really you're just staying safe. At the end of the day, if the activities you're undertaking haven't moved you towards the goal in some way, you're still on that title page, colouring in. Ask, 'What is the purpose of this?' If the honest answer is that you're perfecting, or you're people-pleasing, or being 'badge of honour' busy or you're afraid of failure and don't want to take a risk, it's time to put down those coloured pencils and turn that page …

I WORK BEST UNDER PRESSURE

> I love deadlines. I love the whooshing sound they make as they fly by.
>
> Douglas Adams, *The Salmon of Doubt*

Emma:

'I always do my best work the night before!' my daughter said, crying in the bean bag in my study at home, her fifth huge piece of Year 12 assessment in as many days looming large on the laptop beside her. 'The one time I handed a draft in a week early, I got the same marks I always get!'

'It's not working,' I said, gently.

'It always works! I can't get motivated until I have to!'

Yep. We get it. This old chestnut of thinking you work best under pressure is often the lovechild of a healthy dose of fun distractions and an uninspiring piece of work. At some point along our journey — perhaps at school or university, or in a job early on in our career — we manage to pull a miracle out of our hat by getting something done, to a good standard, the night before and that's it! 'I work best under pressure' becomes entrenched as a belief, and it's easy to entrench it because it comes with a wonderful reward. We get to slack off in the lead-up to getting something finished. We get to do what we want. Getting something done at the last minute is like hanging out with the cool kids: it's a little bit dangerous, a little bit exciting. Risky. It's tantalizing because not only do we get the excitement of manufactured urgency through leaving things late, we get an excuse if it's not brilliant. 'I could have done better, but I literally threw this together in two hours.'

There are two problems with this approach. All you need is for something unexpected to crash your last-minute party and the thrill of the sprint is replaced by genuine stress and panic. You're sick. The kids are sick. Something happens and your one night to get it done is a debacle. You're left under immense strain, or you let someone down. And, even if the night before goes okay and you get the thing finished, those swathes of time while putting it off are never entirely your own. There's always this 'unfinished business', lurking in our minds.

According to psychologist Hal Hershfield from the UCLA Anderson School of Management, people 'tend to fundamentally feel a lack of connection to their future selves'. 'Even though I know on some fundamental level in a year's time I'll still be me,' Hershfield says, 'in some ways I treat that future self as if he's a fundamentally different person, and as if he's not going to benefit or suffer from the consequences of my actions today.' To test this, Hershfield took MRI scans of people while they thought about themselves in the present, then thought about a celebrity like Natalie Portman or Matt Damon, then thought of themselves in the future. Different parts of the brain lit up when people thought about their present and future selves. Interestingly, there was similar brain activity when people described their future self and when they described the celebrity — that's how disconnected we are from ourselves in the future. No wonder we find it so hard to care about the consequences of leaving things for later if our brains aren't even identifying our future selves as us!

Often we allow ourselves to be swept down rabbit holes, such as getting caught up watching videos on YouTube, when we're supposed to be doing something else. We need to stand up and say it, hand on heart: sometimes 'available time' isn't the problem; interest in the task is. And we let our procrastination suck up the time we could spend on things we really want to do, while those interests fade away.

Sometimes it's been so long since we've made time for hobbies or other interests that we've fallen out of love with them, or we can't remember what it feels like to do them or even what they are.

Emma:

When our family was in London a few years ago, we stumbled across a literary festival in Bloomsbury. There was an installation art piece in a park, which comprised a wall of wood panels and some thick black marker pens, along with an invitation for the public to 'graffiti' comments. My then tween seized a pen, drew a love heart and wrote 'I heart Justin Bieber'. Charles Dickens had worked in the house opposite this scene: the cognitive dissonance was overwhelming!

The message that stood out, though, was written in a strong hand in capital letters: 'I'm a banker but I want to be a guitarist.' Who was this person? And what were they doing about this passion?

THERE'S NO TIME FOR HOBBIES!

For five years, every Wednesday night for two or three months of the year, both of us became what was officially known as Offspring Tragics. The TV show *Offspring* is an addictive, off-beat family drama and nothing and nobody got between either of us and that show. That's 66 episodes over five years. Sixty-six hours of our time. In fact, if you include re-watching the boxed set it's actually 132 hours of time (or five and a half days of our lives) that we've devoted to *one* TV show. And that's before we start on *Downton Abbey* and *Outlander* and *I'm A Celebrity, Get Me Out of Here*.

Social media has become so entrenched in our lives it's hard to remember what it was like when there wasn't a temptation to socialize online. It's not unusual to drift to social media and *converse* about how much we have to do, lamenting our lack of time ... while behaving in a way that creates the problem. But remember a time when you first fell in love? You'd move mountains to see that person. You'd meet up, even if it was only for 5 minutes. You'd say no to other things, power through your schoolwork or your work in order to be able to leave on time. You were suddenly completely motivated to be as efficient as is humanly possible. It was easy, then, to prioritize effortlessly because of the incentive to move through the tasks and onto something more enjoyable.

It's only when we have a burning reason to find an extra hour a day for something we love, that the time will magically present itself. It's only then that we'll start to control our use of time, instead of the other way around. It's then that we'll turn off the TV or computer, or say no to other things. It's then that we'll squeeze in our passion around other commitments. The key is lighting that fire in the first place. It's having a reason, other than productivity itself, to be more efficient.

At netball one winter a few years after the experience in Bloomsbury, there was an unfamiliar grandmother sitting on the sidelines. It turned out the reason she hadn't made it to any of the earlier games in the season was because she was having drumming lessons and playing in a garage band on Friday night.

'I've always wanted to!' she said. 'I just had to make it happen!'

Researcher Stuart Brown, MD, describes play as 'time spent without purpose'. Brené Brown said, 'To me this sounds like the definition of an anxiety attack. I feel behind if I'm not using every last moment to be productive, whether that means working, cleaning the house or taking my son to baseball practice. But I can't ignore what the research (mine and others') tells us: play — doing things just because they're fun and not because they'll help achieve a goal — is vital to human development. Play is at the core of creativity and innovation. Play can mean snorkelling, scrapbooking or solving crossword puzzles; it's anything that makes us lose track of time and self-consciousness, creating the clearing where ideas are born.'

THERE'S ONLY ONE CHANCE TO GET THIS RIGHT

Courage is not the absence of fear, but rather the judgment that something else is more important than fear.

Ambrose Redmoon

Audrey:

On a gorgeous, sunny day in late June, I had the privilege of delivering my dad's eulogy. At the time I thought writing it was hard (and it was — I can talk much more easily than I can write) but I felt an unprecedented fear of speaking as I waited to stand up in front of a chapel full of people and speak for 20 minutes about my lovely dad. I felt physically ill and really didn't think I could keep my composure for so long — especially when I had to speak of my mum and dad's great romance, spanning almost six decades.

I've had more than 20 years of training and public speaking experience and though nerves sometimes get the better of me, generally I get through the pre-talk jitters and handle the nervousness. This wasn't about that. I wanted it to be perfect, to capture exactly how my family and I all felt about him and what he brought to our lives. I wanted to do him proud and for my children to hear stories they'd never heard before about their much-adored Poppa.

In the first few minutes of the eulogy, our son, who'd just turned 10, stood beside me and read a short chapter from Dad's book, *Midget Gems*. He was unflappable. On finishing he looked up at me and smiled, and I knew instantly that I could get through Dad's dedication. It was imperfect, it was occasionally slowed by my tears ... and it was real and full of love.

It was the most difficult speech I've ever delivered and also the one for which I'm most grateful. It wasn't until I saw myself and the situation through the eyes of an optimistic and trusting 10-year-old that I regained the perspective I needed in order to do what needed to be done. I realized I could disconnect from the need to get it right and deliver something that wasn't flawless in the way I'd been aiming for, but was flawlessly intentioned and was the highest tribute I could have offered.

Susan Jeffers, author of *Feel the Fear and Do It Anyway*, explains that, 'Every time you encounter something that forces you to "handle it" your self-esteem is raised considerably. You learn to trust that you will survive, no matter what happens. And in this way your fears are diminished immeasurably.'

Some of life's experiences, like delivering a eulogy, can cause us to feel anxious, even when we're able to draw upon our innate skills and abilities. For those who regularly experience anxiety, and who notice it across a number of areas in their lives, there can be a misguided sense of 'weakness'. They watch those around them dealing with life in an easier way — showing up for presentations or interviews, or even for a normal day at work or school and feeling barely ruffled — and they wish they could be so 'courageous'.

Courage is only needed when fear is present. Tackling life with anxiety requires the rousing of much more courage, much more frequently than for people without this added challenge.

Emma:

It was near the end of the second act of the high school musical when I watched as panic started to grip my daughter. This was the same girl who had thrown herself into Act 1 with such spirit and liveliness that the director had asked the ensemble to follow her lead. The stage door was directly behind her and the entire cast was on stage for a big chorus number. No one would notice if she melted through the door and into the cozy folds of the black curtains backstage, out of the spotlight.

By now she was shaking, and feeling nauseous. And dancing and acting and singing so as not to break the visual synchronicity of the performance. She was 'there', but not really 'there'. Her head was spinning, lights and music dazzling as she caught glimpses of the faces in the audience, including mine. She shook her head — a movement so tiny nobody else would have seen it. I nodded mine. The number ended and everyone left the stage, only to return for the finale seconds later. Everyone except my daughter.

That was the third night in a row. Each night, she'd shown up 100 per cent. Each time she'd felt the fear — the sickness and the shakiness caused not by 'stage fright' but by an illness beyond her control — and she'd gone on stage anyway, petrified. To say I was proud is an understatement. There have been years and years before this when she's graced the stage, all smiles and confidence. I was proud then, too — but not like this. Showing up when you feel you can't, braving the 'impossible', doing things while terrified. That's what true courage looks like.

'I thought you'd be disappointed that I didn't finish,' she said. *I didn't get it right.*

'If only you knew how very proud I was that you found the courage to go on at all.'

Putting things off, doing overwhelm and striving for 'perfect' are behaviours that steal our time. Learning to operate more deliberately and efficiently is one of the most empowering ways that we can claw back the time we think we lack, and fill it with the joyful stuff. Easing out of these habits can take some persistence, so begin with our 15-minute experiments and notice the difference not only in the time that opens up, and the sense of order you begin to create, but in how you *feel* when you get things done.

EXPERIMENT 15:
YOUR HEALTH AND WELLBEING
PAY YOURSELF FIRST

With three days until the deadline for submitting this book, Audrey realized she had a routine mammogram booked, which she'd forgotten about. It would have been easy to cancel the appointment, because we hadn't finished the references, hadn't written the acknowledgments and were still inserting the odd paragraph here and there, like this one.

There's almost never a 'convenient time' — particularly for something unpalatable like sticking your boobs into a giant sandwich press in front of a stranger. In fact, justifying putting it off because (eiww, squirm) 50,000 words were due in 72 hours would have been the easiest thing in the world. Surely it was too hard and she should just book the test for another day. She didn't; you're still reading this book, which was submitted on time.

If something isn't scheduled, the chances are it isn't going to happen. Pay yourself first by taking 15 minutes to phone and book the following appointments for the next twelve months, noticing the immediate shift in your sense of empowerment over your health:

* **family doctor — general check-up, plus appointments for your next round of any routine tests (e.g. Pap test, breast check, skin check, heart check)**
* **dentist — for you and your family (next time you're paying for an appointment, schedule the following one at the required interval)**
* **optometrist**
* **any other routine medical appointment that applies to you.**

If you're reading this and thinking, 'I'll do it later', you probably won't. Pick up the phone and work quickly through making the appointments right now — and you'll have set in train the beginnings of a self-care plan for the next 12 months. If you tend to avoid appointments due to fear, consider seeing a psychologist, qualified coach or registered hypnotherapist to work through this to better health.

EXPERIMENT 16: YOUR RELATIONSHIPS LOVE BOMB

Even if it's for only 15 minutes today, let go of busyness and have some fun love bombing! This is a nice, practical task and should be as much fun for you as it is for others. It is half about planning your practical surprise, and half about reflecting on the personalities of the people you care about most.

Author and counsellor Gary Chapman has written about the various ways in which people express love, calling these different forms 'love languages' (see 'References', p. 202). Chapman categorizes our love languages as:

* **acts of service**
* **words of affirmation**
* **receiving gifts**
* **physical touch**
* **quality time.**

For this experiment, reflect on the personality of one of the people closest to you. What would you say is their primary love language? Does one of the above stand out for you when you think of this person? Which surprises or gifts have been best received by them in the past?

Now plan a 'love bomb' for that person, based on their favourite love language. It could be as simple as placing a love note in their lunch box or as complicated as organizing a spontaneous weekend away. At the end of our lives, we'll regret the time we spent putting things off like this, trying to get it 'right' or waiting for a quieter time to do it 'well'.

EXPERIMENT 17:
YOUR CAREER AND BUSINESS
HAVE YOU FINISHED?

Have you noticed that when you're procrastinating on a big task, you tend to 'abandon ship' and focus on smaller and easier things? Researchers Kenneth McGraw and Jirina Fiafa, of the University of Mississippi, found that the biggest challenge to success is often just getting started, and this happens because our brains fear and visualize the very worst aspects of big tasks. The Zeigarnik effect can help. This phenomenon has been observed by psychologists in numerous studies on 'suspense'. People are given a puzzle to complete, but not enough time to finish it. Over 90 per cent of people went back to complete the puzzle even though the experiment was officially over. More than that, they were able to discuss in more detail the incomplete puzzles than the completed ones. Incomplete tasks stay on our minds.

You might have experienced the sensation of getting part of the way through reading a novel or watching a movie and not enjoying it, but finding yourself sticking through until the end, anyway. Putting the book down, half-finished, feels 'wrong' and uncomfortable. We have a desire to complete.

Rather than shelve an entire task for later, start anywhere. Start small. And help to create the momentum you need.

Use the Zeigarnik effect — the human compulsion to finish what you start — by throwing yourself into *any* aspect of a big task that you're putting off, just for 15 minutes. Let go of the need to get it 'right' or 'perfect'. Let go of having to begin at a certain point, or imagining you need more information in order to begin.

This is about starting *before* you're 'ready', starting imperfectly, starting anywhere along the process ... just starting.

The exercise is not about what you produce during this time (that really doesn't matter). It's about opening up the suspense in your mind. This project or task will now be *active.* You've done something towards it, so it's going to be harder to leave it alone because we worry about tasks for which we have not achieved closure. Procrastinating will now become more difficult.

Use this strategy any time you're facing something big and putting it off. By taking the focus off the quality of your work and simply opening the gates and getting into any part of the task, you'll have engaged your brain and it won't want to quit.

EXPERIMENT 18: YOUR FINANCES
BOOK IT IN!

Our intentions for a real escape are often thwarted during the year by a crammed calendar packed with other choices and a bank balance that is committed elsewhere. If you often feel run-down by the end of the year, chances are you're overdue for a proper break.

We can't emphasize enough the benefit of regular time away. As a result of doing this task ourselves a couple of years ago, Emma's family spent a week in Fiji and Audrey's family spent 10 days on Australia's Gold Coast. Highlights of the year!

People who take 'proper holidays' usually plan well ahead.
This is a three-step, 15-minute process:

* **Sit down with your partner or friends, find a suitable date for a break and lock it into your calendar. It doesn't matter if you don't know where you'll go yet — figuring that out later is the fun part!**
* **Email your boss *now* with a request for leave on those dates.**
* **Then open a holiday bank account. You can do this online or over the phone and it will only take a few minutes. Create a direct debit, to transfer funds, no matter how small, into the account weekly, fortnightly or monthly. When we pay ourselves first in time and money, we make wonderful things happen.**

No overthinking! No 'I'll do this later.' Putting off this challenge is how we wind up in a few months' time with 'I desperately need a holiday!' circling on a continuous loop in our minds. Schedule the time, ask for leave, take care of the bank details. Done!

EXPERIMENT 19: YOUR PERSONAL GROWTH THE MOMENTUM MAP™

We each have periods of time where things become unbalanced, peaks and troughs where it's 'all work' or 'all play' (well, maybe it hasn't been 'all play' since we were in primary school, but there are still times in our adult lives that are calmer than others).

For our 'My 15 Minutes' program we created a tool called the Momentum Map™ for people who are tired of tumbling off their own to-do lists and want help to schedule the stuff that matters most. You can download and fill in the Momentum Map™ template from our 'Bonus resources' page at www.my15minutes.com.au/bookbonus, or use the prompts below to create your plan for the week in each of the key areas.

While the list below might look long, each prompt only asks you to do _one_ thing — the idea is to start small and build some momentum into your weekly routine. Try to do these things each week and notice the difference this brings to your life.

THE ONE THING

Choose a 'bang for buck', overarching 'theme' or goal for the week — make it the one thing that, when you accomplish it, will give you a sense of progress.

CONNECT

Date night with a partner or friend? Long-distance phone call? Posting a surprise to a friend? Find one way to connect with people this week.

MOVE IT!

Add one extra physical activity this week. It doesn't matter what, when or how long it takes, just increase your movement a bit!

GROW

Choose to do or engage in one thing that stretches, or even scares, you. Gently push the boundaries of your comfort zone so you're a slightly more experienced person in some way by the end of seven days.

UNPLUG

Discover the 'joy of missing out' by ensuring you spend one hour 'off the grid' each week. Turn off your phone, computer and devices — don't just put them on silent, but turn them off.

RECHARGE

Whether you're introverted or extroverted, spend a little time topping up your energy in the best way you know how.

RELEASE

What we 'ditch' makes a huge difference in our lives. What's one thing you're prepared to release or let go? It could be a physical item, or a habit, choice, behaviour or thought.

APPRECIATE

Gratitude is the antidote to fear. Each week, write down one thing you're grateful for and you'll create a new pattern of looking for the good.

EXPERIMENT 20: YOUR HOME
TACKLE THAT HOT SPOT

You know that feeling of bliss after you've finished cleaning your entire home? Everything in its place, surfaces clean, benches and taps sparkling? This 'showroom state' of household perfection rarely lasts long — particularly when you throw kids into the mix. As a result, sometimes when we glance at the house as a whole, we feel an overall sense of 'Gah!' Achieving that goal of being completely on top of everything can feel out of reach, so we might choose to do nothing.

As with most big challenges, this is because we tend to view the job as a whole, rather than in achievable baby steps. It isn't about attaining perfection — it's about understanding that we don't need to get *everything right* for it to make a difference.

Choose a room and identify a 'hot spot' (we're not talking wireless internet here, we're talking cluttered surfaces, piles of things, items in completely the wrong place or room etc.).

Set a timer and go like a 'bat out of hell' in that hot spot for 15 minutes.

If you find that you've blitzed the hot spot in under the designated 15 minutes, move on to a second hot spot in the same room, until the timer beeps!

Remember: the purpose of this task is to educate yourself on how much can be accomplished at home in a 15-minute block of time. Understanding this can remove that sense of overwhelm and need for perfection that you might have been experiencing.

EXPERIMENT 21: YOUR FUN AND RECREATION
DO SOMETHING (YOU THINK) YOU'RE HOPELESS AT

At some point in your life, everything was new. Primary school. High school. Work. Relationships. Completing your tax return. There was a time when even the most ordinary, everyday things had never been done before. And now you do them, often mindlessly, without issue.

We often put pressure on ourselves to do things well, or even 'perfectly'. We can loosen this up by giving ourselves permission to be beginners.

Choose an activity that is new to you, in which you're not invested at all (that is, it really doesn't matter to you whether you succeed or fail — it's only for fun). Perhaps it's making a soufflé, rock-climbing or singing karaoke, making some pottery or riding a skateboard.

Throw yourself in, laugh and enjoy your clumsy attempts as a 'newbie'. Who knows — you might find you're a natural!

BEFORE WE MOVE ON ...

You must love yourself before you love another. By accepting yourself and fully being what you are, your simple presence can make others happy. You yourself, as much as anybody in the entire universe, deserve your love and affection.

Buddha

As babies, we come into the world with only two fears — fear of falling and fear of loud noises. We're not born worrying that if we try to stand and take some steps, we might stumble while people are watching. When we're babies, we don't care if we stumble once or a hundred times. We don't mind who sees it, either. It's just ourselves and the goal, with no yawning chasm of fear, shame and the private and very 'adult' freak-out: 'What if this doesn't work?'

A little later, though, we learn the truth: there are things you can't do, no matter how much you want to or how hard you try. There are people who might laugh at you when you fall. As we stumble to make sense of a world that's harsher than we first thought, fear starts shaping our choices. As fun as it was to 'fly by the seat of our pants' it's actually safer standing a little further back from the edge.

When Dannielle Miller was a toddler, she was badly burnt. She grew up to be Australia's leading educator on teen body image and confidence, CEO of Enlighten Education and a best-selling author of several books for teen girls about body image, growing up and 'lovability'. We interviewed her in 2014 and share her thoughts about perfection.

As such a little girl, only two, I was so badly hurt. I was a very sick little girl. They didn't think I would survive. I was in hospital for six months. It's often the shock that will kill you. The next major complication is infection ...

The scars didn't worry me at all. I was this bossy, busy little girl who thought she would rule the empire. I continued with my love of books and of reading, and powerful princess stories and the Secret Seven. But by the time I was about thirteen, things really shifted ... and I suppose that's why I have such empathy with teen girls. I thought no one would ever love me because of my scars and I thought that I wouldn't make friends because of them. The more I hid, the more it felt like this big, dark secret.

I realized my value was not just my body — that there were many things about me that were beautiful and would make me loveable. I realized I had to be a good role model. I had to step up and show them that I was enough.

I often say to teen girls, 'What do you think it will be like to be a woman?' and they say, 'It doesn't look like much fun. Mum tells me I'm beautiful, but I know she doesn't think she is.' Girls can't be what they can't see. If we don't show them that they're enough, then they're not going to believe that they are, either.

I've met CEOs of incredible companies — multi-million-dollar global companies and they will say to me, 'Danni, I know I'm a powerful, together woman, but I still can't help but feel guilty every time I eat a chocolate biscuit.' It's such a liberating thing when you let go of that.

My scars have become something that I wear as a badge of honour, and I think all the cool superheroes have a story, or a scar … mine are more visible, but we all carry scars. And it's whether we choose to embrace those or let them burden us that matters.

Perfection, overwhelm, procrastination, doing it all yourself, fearing failure … these all squeeze our available time. Another mindset that gets in our way is the sense that we're stuck or trapped. It's the belief that there's no way out, or that a situation can't be changed. This can cause inertia, or lead us to stay in unsatisfying situations much longer than we need to, through fear, confusion, stubbornness or lack of knowledge.

MINDSET GREMLIN 4

WHEN YOU'RE FEELING STUCK (BUT YOU'RE NOT)

The beliefs listed below all relate to feeling as though a situation can't be changed. How many of these beliefs ring true for you?

BELIEVE IT OR NOT?

- ☐ I can't leave my job and start a new business. Everyone would be horrified.
- ☐ Maybe I should be a stay-at-home mum. Everyone I grew up with judges me for working.
- ☐ I have to stay at work late whether there's work to do or not. It's the culture.
- ☐ I know our marriage isn't ideal, but I'm staying for the children.
- ☐ This could mean exposure or attention. I don't like being in the spotlight.
- ☐ I should have a life plan and pursue it with focus — but I don't.

- ☐ I wish my brain could think more quickly and I could be wittier and more eloquent.
- ☐ I am the only one who doesn't get this.
- ☐ What's the point? No one cares!
- ☐ I think I overload myself.

A LESSON FROM THAILAND

Sometimes we limit ourselves with a belief that there's only one way to do things. In striving to follow that path, we miss the opportunities we have to create a life we'd love more. And, of course, it's often that familiar battle between risk and security that traps us.

We met a woman once in a workshop who told us a remarkable story of breaking out of the future that was expected for her and creating a new one. She explained that her family had had a tough year and, to recover and 're-group', they'd packed up and gone on a holiday to Thailand for Christmas. It was 2004, and in an unexpected, traumatic twist of fate their family was one of hundreds of thousands who found themselves in the path of the Boxing Day tsunami. Miraculously, they survived but nothing was the same for them afterwards — particularly for the 16-year-old girl, who was intending to return from their 'holiday' and begin the final two years of her schooling.

Her subject choices were already picked: everything that would best help her tertiary entrance score. Physics, chemistry, double-major maths …

'I'm changing all of them!' she announced on their return. 'I want to do double music and dance and art and history.'

Cue panic from her parents and teachers. 'We know you've been through a life-threatening experience, but don't throw your life away because of it!'

She stuck to her guns, though, and changed her subjects to the ones that lit her up and, two years later, surprised them all with a near perfect final score.

'Right!' everyone pounced. 'You can't waste a score like that! Do law! Do medicine! Do …'

'I want to be a songwriter,' she announced. 'And a country music singer.'

Everyone reeled.

Galvanized by her intuition and determination, she ignored the advice again and went on to study music and philosophy. She wrote songs and performed, which led her to performing in Nashville, like she'd always dreamed.

It's not always other people's expectations that box us in or narrow our path. Sometimes it's our own. We fall into a rut of 'this is how I always do it'. We cling to an established process out of habit, certainty or comfort. We adopt unhelpful perspectives on situations, or we think that preserving the status quo seems more important than making progress another way. We like to reinforce that we're 'right' and back up our decisions. It pains us to admit we made mistakes. Pioneer computer scientist, Rear Admiral Grace Hopper, knew this when she said, 'The most damaging phrase in the language is: "It's always been done that way"'. We're going to look now at what happens when we feel stuck, and how we can take steps to get 'unstuck' and create our own momentum.

I CAN'T LET PEOPLE DOWN

Audrey:

When I'd just turned 30 and was recently single, I was living a comfortable life in a new home, with a secure job and a great social life. The world was my oyster — or would have been had I *actually left* my comfortable suburban existence to go fishing.

A group of friends were planning a big trip to Bali and I was an assumed part of the cohort. But something was holding me back. It's not that I didn't want to go away, and certainly not that I didn't want to spend time with these old friends. Something about the idea just didn't 'gel'.

I was having dinner with another friend the Saturday before the Monday deadline for a final 'yes' or 'no'.

Frustratingly, I was still flip-flopping. I wanted to travel but I didn't want to go to Bali. Not going to Bali would mean I was letting my friends down — something I really didn't want to do.

'Why don't you just go somewhere else?' my friend suggested objectively. 'Why not the UK or Europe?'

That was it. By the Sunday night I was on the phone to my lovely friend, Lainey, who had been living in London for several months. She threw another curve-ball into the mix — how about heading over to London for a 12-month working holiday? Easy.

By Tuesday I'd resigned from my job. By Thursday I'd bought a one-way ticket to Heathrow. By Sunday I'd told all of my family and friends I was going away for a year. Within a month I'd organized to lease my home to tenants.

Two months later I was living in London.

Six *years* later, and with a new career, new friends, new husband and a baby on the way, I finally came home.

There have been several times in both our lives when we've felt trapped by others' expectations. (Most times, however, our response isn't as drastic as to pack up everything we own and move to the other side of the world!) Each time, we were on a certain path, committed to something that wasn't working or we were stuck in a situation without a clear way out. It felt suffocating, scary and miserable.

For longer than we should have, we stayed on those paths. It wasn't until we found ourselves envisaging awful scenarios as potential 'solutions' that we realized just how bad things were. You know the kind of extreme, life-sabotaging, ridiculously unrealistic daydreams that we mean? We had a conversation about this form of Extreme People Pleasing (the type where you're so scared to put on your Big Girl Pants and speak up assertively to get yourself out of something, that you bargain with the universe about weird stuff happening instead). We asked the members in our program about this kind of thinking, many of whom understood exactly where we were coming from and had experienced similar thoughts:

- → 'Maybe I'll get the flu and won't have to go to that party.'
- → 'Maybe if I have a minor car accident — just enough to need crutches — I'll have a good enough reason to leave the job my boss won't let me quit.'
- → 'Maybe the building will burn down then I won't have to go to work.'
- → 'Maybe if I stay in this relationship long enough, time will pass, the decision will be taken out of my hands and I won't have to let anyone down.'

When we're feeling this desperate and our daydreams have taken a darker turn, it's time to rescue ourselves. In our own situations, we realized we weren't as powerless as we felt and that things didn't have to stay as they were. There were ways out that didn't involve waiting for dire circumstances to conspire in our 'favour' and sort life out the 'easy way'. As confronting as that felt at the time, and as riddled with 'pros and cons' as the solution seemed, we could untangle these situations ourselves.

What that involved, before anything else, was recognizing self-worth. Staying trapped can feel easier than finding a way out. Better the devil you know ... Letting ourselves down is painful, but in so many ways it seems easier than letting others down.

Other people factor in your life story. Some
are key characters in it. Those closest to
you may take up entire chapters — but
they are not the whole book, and nor are
they the hero in the story. Most of us would
walk away desperately disappointed in a
movie in which the lead character failed to
overcome obstacles, prioritized everyone
else and chose the back seat in her own
life. Yet that's the storyline that plays out so
often in reality.

When a friend's marriage fell apart she wrote a social media post thanking her friends for support. The reason she'd stuck with an unhappy situation so long was precisely because of her continued prioritization of other people above herself. Those who might criticize your choices do not live inside your life. They do not live inside your heart. When you lie awake at night agonizing over your situation, they are soundly asleep. Sometimes when someone makes a brave decision to leave something (a career, a relationship, a country) others feel threatened by it. Sometimes they're threatened because they're not strong enough to make the harder choice themselves.

Swimming against your own current is exhausting. The slogging. The straining. The *pretending*. Trying to live a life that isn't really 'yours', just to avoid letting other people down, is a decision to value others' lives more highly than your own. The ironic thing is that in all but a few key cases, many of the people who would dictate your choices now — whose input feels so vital — will have drifted from your life in a few years' time.

It's not about ignoring all advice. It's about turning up the volume of your own intuition and listening to those who are able to guide you impartially. Surrendering to your own current is liberating. Being who you really are and going where you really want to go brings a beautiful blend of passion and peace. Turning things around isn't always easy, and often there's 'no way out but through'. That 'through way' can be some of the hardest territory you'll ever cross, but it's not quite as hard as staying where you are in the long term.

THIS ALWAYS HAPPENS

> Life is 10 per cent what you make it and 90 per cent how you take it.
>
> Irving Berlin

Sometimes it's not so much the situation that is the stumbling block, but our attitude towards it. The filter of optimism or pessimism that we apply in any experience changes the way we respond to it which, in turn, changes the results we achieve.

Emma:

Maybe it's my Irish heritage, but I'm always on the lookout for 'signs'. Signs that I'm on the right track with something, or that things will work out. Positive vibes. Serendipitous coincidences. So, when my colleague, composer Sally Whitwell, and I were taking our first tentative steps out of cloud storage with our musical based on my teen novel, *Unrequited: Girl meets boy band* — something to which we'd passionately dedicated an entire summer of late nights — I wanted *signs*. Good ones! And lots of them! The musical was being featured at a music-theatre event in Sydney called Broadway Unplugged. Oh. My. Goodness. Nerve-wracking!

Well! The signs came thick and fast. We had difficulty with a ticketing issue and an unsettling conversation with a member of staff. Returning to the car after the performance, we found a $106 parking ticket for facing the wrong way to the kerb. On the same day, this ticket was unfortunately joined by my first ever speeding ticket, for driving 10 kilometres over the limit on an unfamiliar road. We got lost on the way out of the city, and then we found the highway McDonald's had shut up shop minutes before we rolled into its car park after midnight on the way home, hoping for an injection of caffeine.

What could it have all meant, Mulder? Could coming up against obstacle after obstacle have meant we were on the wrong track with the musical? Should we have cut our losses?

Well, it could have meant that, I suppose, if we'd chosen to focus on that stuff instead of swatting each of those irritants away with a sigh and a 'move on!' And if we'd dwelled on everything that went wrong that day, we wouldn't have noticed these ...

Sign 1: The lead character in the story, Kat, sings in the chorus of the Sydney University Theatre Company's production of the *Legally Blonde* musical, held at a theatre called the Seymour Centre. Driving past the Seymour Centre, we noticed the Sydney University Theatre Company was, right then, staging *Legally Blonde*.

Sign 2: Sally recounted the story of walking past the same theatre, only to see a young woman run out of it in tears, followed by someone else calling after her, yelling, 'Kat! Kat!'

Sign 3: This is our favourite! I was stopped directly outside the door of the theatre where our show was to be featured, by a little old lady with a walking stick, who wanted to admire my umbrella. It's only then that I noticed she was wearing a One Direction T-shirt (the band that inspired the book when my daughter wasn't a fan of reading, but *was* a fan of Harry Styles).

We tend to zero in on anything that supports our current obsession. The more we look for 'signs', the more we'll see. We had plenty of obstacles that day, but the goal was brighter, and searching for evidence to back that up was more productive than sinking into a funk.

We don't get this right all the time. We've run stories in our minds to support a strategy that's not working, because it's easier than changing what we're doing and fixing the situation. It's so simple to find the evidence we're looking for, and so easy to filter out information that clashes with a belief we're holding onto.

AN EXPERIMENT WITH PURPLE FEATHERS

When Emma and her three best school friends turned 40, they went away for a long weekend. They had a copy of a book by Pam Grout called *E-Squared: Nine do-it-yourself energy experiments that prove your thoughts create your reality*, which contains a series of fun experiments designed to prove that this stuff works. One of the experiments demands you count how many purple feathers you see in a 24-hour period.

Purple feathers? Who's ever seen *one* in their entire lives, let alone more than one? Pfft!

Not two hours later, during a fireside viewing of *The Importance of Being Earnest* on DVD, out swished Dame Judi Dench, resplendent in an elaborate purple outfit, heavily accessorized with a hat *exploding* with purple feathers! What's more, the next morning, wandering the craft markets in a local village, shop after shop contained purple-feather-themed wares: dream-catchers, mobiles, scarves, hats, paintings … Where the expectation had been to see not one purple feather, the reality was there were hundreds!

Audrey, having read the same book on a camping trip, experimented with looking for yellow butterflies. The family was about to do a three-hour highway drive at the time, so nobody was optimistic. Sure enough, as they drove at walking pace out of the camping ground minutes after settings themselves the task, they looked out the window only to see a yellow butterfly flying beside them, keeping pace with their car.

Any time we decide to focus consciously on something, we'll see it. A new word we've only just heard seems repeated several times in different conversations the next week, on TV, in ads — everywhere. Develop a new interest in a particular model of car and the roads will be full of it. Likewise, the evidence that would disprove our entrenched beliefs is always there. It's just a matter of consciously looking for it. Why is this important? Because a belief like 'It's probably not even possible' or 'This always happens!' or 'Nothing ever goes right' can stop us from having a go at fabulous things.

Another way we limit ourselves is by giving up early, thinking we've tried everything.

I THOUGHT THERE WAS NO OTHER WAY

> Mum is always worrying what other people think. Bugger other people!
>
> Emma's grandfather, Bill

Audrey:

My dad was a man of many passions but perhaps the most challenging and inspiring was his love of marathon running. Some may say that he wasn't ideally built for his chosen sport — he certainly didn't have a frame resembling an Olympic athlete — but he had the stamina, strength and above all steel tenacity to complete 31 full marathons, including the prestigious London marathon, twice.

Dad's greatest sporting achievement was his participation in an ultra-triathlon in 1988. This was a six-day event involving cycling, kayaking and running 600 kilometres through South Australia. His dedication to his rigorous training plan for the ultra-tri and his focus on the ultimate goal was awe inspiring. It just was not in his nature to give up — a trait which was evident until the very end of his life.

On the fifth day of the event, Dad had run an ultra-marathon — 63 kilometres. The final day was 42.2 kilometres — a full marathon through the Adelaide Hills and finishing in the city. Five kilometres into the race, Dad met with a small pothole in the road and fell in a heap on the ground, badly damaging a tendon in his knee. That should have been it, but he would not let the injury beat him. He soon realized that he couldn't walk down even the slightest gradient without a considerable amount of pain, but in order to finish this race he needed to make it down one of Adelaide's steepest, winding roads, known as Devil's Elbow, which was as challenging as it sounds. So Dad did the only thing that any crazy, devoted marathon runner would do — he walked mile after mile backwards!

During the lonely moments in the depths of childbirth it can feel as if everything's going to go wrong. Despite having a supporting cast of family and medical people in the room, you can feel completely alone, thinking, 'Nobody can get me out of this, but me.' At that classic moment where women start begging to go home, they find the strength from somewhere. They have to get the job done. So they push. Once. Twice. An hour's worth. Two hours' worth. More …

The human spirit has a desire to get through. We might love shortcuts, and we might love the easy way, for things to be straightforward and achievable. A magic solution would be fabulous. But sometimes a challenge requires us to dig deeper and step up further than we ever have before, often under pressure, and into new things. Despite how daunting and terrifying this might seem, even some of the biggest dilemmas — the ones that are seemingly insurmountable — are still just about solving one problem and then the next. One push. Another push.

THIS SITUATION CANNOT BE CHANGED

God grant me the serenity
to accept the things I cannot change,
The courage
to change the things I can
And the wisdom
to know the difference.

Reinhold Niebuhr

Lisa LaMaitre wrote about her experience of childlessness:

_____

Over the last five years I've couched my words, limited my language. 'We're trying to have a baby' (although to me this translates as 'not trying hard enough!'). 'We're focused on babies' (means we're spending a lot of time in the bedroom without any results). 'The doctors say I have endometriosis' (is my way of assuring myself that I have the power to change this diagnosis, if I simply don't own it). What I do have to own, though, is at the tender age of 44, and after 19 years of marriage to

the man I love, we still don't have children
of our own. And this is something that I
desperately, do not want to own.

There are times when we feel stuck in hard places from which escape
might be difficult, but it is at least possible. And there are a handful
of situations we would do anything not to have to face, from which
'escape' is not possible. Childlessness, accident, injury and illness, the
deaths of those we love, even unrequited love are all situations in
which we might find ourselves unexpectedly trapped, feeling lost and
powerless.

Being trapped in an unchangeable situation pushes us towards
human limits we didn't know existed. We can be stretched further than
we thought possible. And for Lisa, that meant finding other ways to
mother and to nurture those around her. For her it wasn't just throwing
herself into the role of aunt; she has created a large circle of women
who gather to inspire and support each other.

Like the tiny plant that pushes up through the cracks in thick
concrete, people seem to do something super-human as they push
up through grief, loss and disappointment and carve a new path.
But that can take time, as explained to us by Stacey Copas, aspiring
Paralympian athlete and author of *How to Be Resilient: The blueprint
for getting results when things don't go to plan*:

When things do go wrong, it can feel like
it's the end of the world. But it does open
up incredible opportunities if we allow it
to. It's a decision we make: are we going to
let it hold us back, or will it be something
we use to leverage us to bigger and better
things. The biggest issue most of us have is

that we get in our own way.

It was the first weekend of summer. It was a very hot afternoon and my brother and I went over for a swim. I kept diving in over and over again. Being yelled at to stop didn't deter me. I stood on the edge of the pool and the perfectionist in me thought, 'How can I make this the perfect dive?' … It seemed like any other dive until I went to swim up to the surface and I realized I couldn't move …

My life as I knew it was over. That split-second decision really changed my life forever. I was getting yelled at: 'Stop doing that! You'll break your neck.' You're invincible at that age.

'It wasn't until I was in my twenties that I realized that what had happened was a blessing. That it had changed my life in a positive way. What changed for me is that I just don't take things for granted. There is a greater appreciation for life itself and for the things you can do. The things that I've done with my life I can say with certainty I would not have done — it completely changed my journey in a way that has been

far more rewarding and enjoyable.
I've come across so many people
who think the world is over.
It's grieving for the life that you had,
but it's important to tap into the potential
that people have.
I'm just so grateful that the experience I've
had has had an impact on others.

I've had to get over myself and that's the
biggest issue we have because we get in
our own way.

When I had my accident
I made a pact with myself that I was never
going to do any sport again because I
couldn't do it like I used to. I kept that up
for 22 years, which is sheer madness. Just
after my 34th birthday I thought it might be
a good time to get fit. Then I got a letter
in the mail from the Paralympic committee
saying that I displayed all the physical
attributes to be a potential Paralympian.
The big thing was that realization that
before my accident I was never going to be
good enough to compete and represent
my country ... all those years I didn't think
I was good enough.

It's never too late. It's only too late if you've decided it's too late. Starting some of these things later, we have a massive advantage because we've got a lot of that life experience. The mindset is there.

_____

EXPERIMENT 22:
YOUR HEALTH AND WELLBEING
LEAN IN TO JOY

Brené Brown speaks of that sense of foreboding that we sometimes feel about our children — that we are so lucky and privileged to have them, yet we see them sleeping peacefully and suddenly have a terrible sense that everything is going to be snatched away from us. Whether we have children or not, this can be applied to any situation or person to which we are deeply attached.

Consider these statistics, published by Earl Nightingale:

→ 40 per cent of the things we worry about never happen

→ 30 per cent of the things we worry about have already happened

→ 12 per cent of our worries are needless worries, such as what someone else thinks about us

→ 10 per cent of our worries are unimportant or petty, such as what's for dinner, being late or what to wear

→ 8 per cent of our worries actually happen (4 per cent are things beyond our control, while 4 per cent are things we can control, such as the outcome of our decisions).

Spend a few minutes writing a list of all of the worries, concerns or anxious thoughts with which you are currently dealing. Be sure just to 'dump' all of these on your list without judgment or priority.

Next, using the guide below, classify each of your current concerns into one of the five categories:

    * **things that have already happened and cannot be changed**

    * **needless worries (e.g. what someone thinks of you)**

* petty and unimportant worries (e.g. what to wear, being late, what's for dinner)
* situations that are likely to occur but over which you have *no* influence (e.g. getting sick, death of a loved one, natural disasters)
* situations over which you *do* have control.

Notice any wasted time and energy being spent on situations that are in the past or are beyond your influence. Complete this task by focusing now only on the issues over which you do have influence, and write a list of actions you can take to improve those situations.

EXPERIMENT 23: YOUR RELATIONSHIPS
PICK YOUR BATTLES

If you're like us, every so often you decide to 'get your act together' and transform a heap of areas in your life in one hit. It's the typical 'New Year's resolution' approach and it tends not to work in the long term because it's overwhelming to change several aspects at once.

In the same way, it's too much to expect people around us to improve their behaviour in all areas at once. For example, a parent of a teenager might decide that this term, the child will focus on studying more and improving their marks. It may matter less if their room is tidy. Someone with a toddler might focus for now on nice manners and carrying empty plates to the sink but choose to overlook needing matching clothes. It could be that you've expressed a need for change in some aspects of your relationship with your partner or a friend. It may be as simple as remembering to put out the rubbish bin or preparing the dinner without being asked.

At every stage, there will be things that matter more and things that matter less. One of the most beneficial changes we can make in our relationships is to gain some clarity on this and let some things go.

Spend 15 minutes 'picking your battles'. Write a list of all of the things that currently frustrate you about the behaviour of others, then circle the ones that matter most. Cross off the behaviours that matter less and decide to let them go. It really is that simple.

EXPERIMENT 24:
YOUR CAREER AND BUSINESS
YOU'RE ONE OF A KIND!

It's the pesky Inner Critic who often jostles to centre stage, grabs a microphone inside our heads and dictates the self-talk. Finger-pointing at faults and failures often becomes the well-rehearsed script, and our confidence can be shaken by it.

Each of us offers more to our work than what's contained in our job description. Think more broadly than the performance of your set tasks — about other ways that you enhance your workplace, the working lives of your colleagues or clients and the success of the organization.

Looking back on the past working year, hit back at any self-flagellation by writing down a list of fifteen reasons your team or clients are lucky to have you. Your list might include things like being the person in whom people confide at work when things go wrong, the one who never forgets a birthday or someone who praises others' efforts. Maybe you're the diplomat during heated meetings, the one who organizes team sport at lunchtimes or someone who helps others see the bright side of bad news. Once you've made your list, take some time to appreciate your contributions.

EXPERIMENT 25: YOUR FINANCES
WHEN LESS IS MORE

Have you ever stood in front of a cashier searching frantically for that elusive $10 in your purse? You know it's in there but you need to sift through dozens of receipts in order to find it. It's so frustrating that you finally give in and pay by credit or debit card just to avoid the glares of the people around you. Yep, we've both been there and done that.

An overstuffed wallet can be more than just annoying, though. What would happen if your wallet was lost or stolen — would you have easy access to any emergency funds? It can also contribute to a feeling of chaos and overwhelm in relation to our finances. It's time to organize your wallet to make life easier.

In 15 minutes, do the following:

* **Clean out any unwanted receipts from your wallet.**
* **Donate small change to the nearest fundraiser, or pop the coins into a money box (tip: always keep some coins in your car, out of sight, for parking meters).**

* **Remove any identifying information from your wallet other than your driver's licence and healthcare cards (do not carry PIN, account numbers etc.).**
* **Ensure that you have emergency contact details in your wallet, and create an ICE (In Case of Emergency) contact in your phone (there are smartphone apps for this).**
* **Copy or scan all cards and file the information somewhere safe — there are some great smartphone apps, many of which you can buy with your loose change!**
* **If you have two or more credit cards, keep one in your wallet and the others at home (for access to funds if your wallet is lost or stolen).**

* Aim to carry $25 to $50 cash at all times (enough to split a restaurant bill with friends, but not so much that the loss would hurt).

EXPERIMENT 26: YOUR PERSONAL GROWTH
CREATE A MEMORY JAR AND START A NEW TRADITION

So many of our experiences are recorded online these days and, in the digital age, we tend to have fewer tangible objects than previous generations to remind us of our happy times.

When you're having a bad day, it can be uplifting to read through something good from the past and remind yourself that it's just a bad 'day' — not a bad 'life'.

Find a glass jar or even an unused vase and create a label for this year (e.g. Happy Days). Whenever something uplifting or happy unfolds, take 30 seconds to jot it down on a piece of paper (coloured sticky notes would be great, or create your own memory notes or cards), fold it up and place the memory into the jar. Encourage

others in your family to add their own memories to the jar. At the end of the calendar year or even on New Year's Eve, sit down with the family and take it in turns to read through and re-live the times that brought you brightness.

The mere act of paying attention when good things happen will be beneficial for developing an optimistic perspective. If you're always on the lookout for positive anecdotes to add to the jar, you'll notice more and more of the good things that exist already in your life. What we focus on, we attract. You may also wish to pop in little notes of appreciation when you see family members doing something thoughtful — imagine their surprise when they realize you noticed, and how much it meant to you.

EXPERIMENT 27: YOUR HOME
USE IT OR LOSE IT

Sometimes we can experience a sense of overwhelm simply by entering our own home. We walk in the door and feel the burden of 'stuff'. It may be cluttered, needing a good clean or just simply messy. Regardless, we can feel in need of a fairy godmother or a magical elf who can transform our home at the swish of a wand or the click of a finger.

Most of us have items in our homes that we keep because we feel we should. Perhaps they were unwanted gifts, or things that were once expensive to buy but we've never really used or liked. Keeping these things drags us down and prevents us from enjoying spacious, uncluttered living.

Spend 15 minutes walking through your house and gathering up a pile of items that you're holding onto *not* because you like them or use them, but for some other reason. For each item, ask yourself, 'Is this adding to my lifestyle or taking from it?' Let go of anything that is dragging you down, and make room for lightness and space.

Remember, anything that only ever comes out of the cupboard during spring cleaning can probably be donated.

Either use it or lose it!

EXPERIMENT 28: YOUR FUN AND RECREATION
GET SOME PERSPECTIVE

One of the most popular tasks in the 'fun and recreation' category of the 'My 15 Minutes' program involves spending 15 minutes lying on the grass, looking up at the sky through the trees. We've loved seeing the private Facebook group buzz with photos of people's unique views on 'their' sky, and comments about how tranquil and grounding the experience felt. It reminded many of us of what we used to do as kids, back when we had all the time in the world …

Here's a spin on that powerful 'looking up' task, and it's perfect for when we're preoccupied with everything that we have to do and are feeling wrapped up in our own little worlds.

Spend 15 minutes, after dark, lying in your driveway, on your front lawn, or in the backyard, staring at the night sky. Do this alone, or with a partner or friends. Keep your eye out for shooting stars … you never know.

This task is about taking some time out and appreciating the universe — and it may also act as a 'galactic filter' which will help you to sift out the worries that are causing you disproportionate angst. While you're lying there, looking up, ask yourself what really matters to you right now.

BEFORE WE MOVE ON ...

Emma:

'Just letting you know that Mal will be at my book launch tomorrow,' my husband said to me about three years back, 'but he'll be there as Catherine.'

It took me a few seconds to grasp what he meant. Malcolm McGregor — then speechwriter to the Australian Chief of Army, including a speech on the treatment of women in the army that went viral internationally for all the right reasons, but, more importantly, our little boy's godfather and one of my husband's best mates — was now living as a woman.

My husband had known for about six months and had respected Catherine's request for privacy. Gender transition after spending a lifetime feeling trapped in the wrong body is a situation of an emotional and physical magnitude that most of us never have to fathom.

'I was waiting for somebody to say, here, take this pill, and it will all be fine,' Catherine told the *Australian Women's Weekly*, speaking of a conversation with her psychiatrist. 'And he said, "It won't be fine. Can't you see that?" I said, "But I'm an infantry officer, I'm married, it's too late, I'm 50-something years old, it's not an option." He said, "I'm puzzled you've got this far."'

In my first email exchange with Catherine the night before my husband's book launch (which was also one of Catherine's earliest 'official' appearances as a female), I reassured her of my full support. I'll never forget her response, which was one of relief, but she also gave us an 'out' if we wanted her to step down as godparent for our son.

When you think about the kind of adults you want as role models in your kids' lives, there's usually a 'wish list' of qualities. For me, it's someone who'll stand up for what they believe in, and who'll be themselves even when the world seems against them. I want someone who'll take risks and act with integrity, authenticity and compassion. In Catherine's case, we had all of that plus one of the sharpest, most articulate and funny minds I think I've ever encountered. Why would we sack her as godparent?

Since then, we've watched as she 'came out' as a transgendered person. We've seen her navigate media interviews with poise and openness. We've seen her give interviews on TV and radio, and in the print and online media — each one more impressive and confident than the last. We've seen her combat online trolls and respond to a barrage of transphobia. We've watched her learn when to engage and when to maintain a dignified silence. We've seen her do all of this while working in two very male-dominated professional arenas — the military and the world of cricket. And we've seen people in both of those male-dominated and 'traditional' realms respond to her with almost overwhelming positivity.

Catherine became the highest ranking transgendered military officer in the world. She remains a well-respected political and cricket commentator. As much as I deeply respect the career aspects (she's incredibly talented to the point of mind-blowing in her grasp of complex situations), for me it's always the personal qualities that matter most.

There are some situations from which it is far easier to extract ourselves than others. There are some situations where the grief and pain are raw, and where our priority must be personal survival and the welfare of those around us. But there are other situations that, while they seem dire, can be changed.

Getting 'unstuck' from a situation like Catherine faced, from which there genuinely and 'for eternity' seemed no escape, is an example so extreme it can jolt us from our own perspective. Is there *really* no other option for us? Is there *really* no way out, or no different approach that we can take? Or are we staying stuck to save ourselves from other things: taking action that feels uncomfortable or distressing, displeasing people, feeling as though we're being judged for our choices …

Or could it be another mindset gremlin altogether?

MINDSET GREMLIN 5

WHEN YOU THINK IT'S TOO LATE (BUT IT ISN'T)

How many of the following beliefs about fear of change, or fear of success, resonate with you?

BELIEVE IT OR NOT?

- [ ] If I get promoted my job won't be as flexible and I won't be able to spend as much time with my kids.
- [ ] Will I be able to handle a bigger/brighter spotlight? Will I become even more overwhelmed?
- [ ] My friends won't like me as much if I succeed.
- [ ] Successful people don't have time for their loved ones.
- [ ] I'm scared I'll get what I want and then not be able to handle it.
- [ ] If I succeed, then what?
- [ ] I don't want to be in the limelight because I'm scared of being criticized.
- [ ] If I'm successful, people will be jealous.

- [ ] If I get pregnant, I'll be out of my depth. What if I'm not a good mother?
- [ ] If I fall in love, I might lose myself.

LESSONS FROM EVERYWHERE

Dame Helen Mirren didn't achieve real acclaim until she was cast as Jane Tennison in *Prime Suspect*, at the age of 45. 'There are a privileged few,' she said, 'who just seem to waft through life without ever having to meet any adversity … The rest of us, we have to struggle and fight. Sometimes you have to do stuff you're not familiar with or think you'll fail horribly at. You just have to jump in the deep end.' She jumped. And bagged her first Oscar at 61.

She's in great company. How's this for an honour roll of late bloomers who pushed through initial rejection and found success later in life:

→ Walt Disney was fired from the *Kansas City Star* because his editor thought he 'lacked imagination and had no good ideas'.

→ Steven Spielberg was rejected multiple times by the University of Southern California School of Cinematic Arts.

→ Oprah Winfrey was fired from her first TV gig for getting 'too emotionally invested in her stories'.

→ Vera Wang originally wanted to be an Olympic figure skater but failed to make the team. She became an editor at *Vogue* but was passed over for the editor-in-chief position before starting to design wedding dresses at 40.

→ Colonel Sanders was fired dozens of times and travelled across the United States looking for someone to sell his fried chicken before finally getting a business deal at age 65 (legend has it he heard 1009 'no's' before his first 'yes').

→ Before R.H. Macy established one of the largest department store chains in the world, he had a series of failed retail ventures.

→ Thomas Edison's teachers told him he was 'too stupid to learn anything'. He was fired from his first two jobs for not being productive.

- → For one of Fred Astaire's first screen tests, an executive wrote of him, 'Can't sing. Can't act. Slightly balding. Can dance a little.'
- → J.K. Rowling was a single mum living off welfare when she began writing the first novel in the Harry Potter series, which received twelve rejections before going on to make her the world's first billionaire author.
- → Van Gogh only sold one painting in his lifetime, just months before his death.
- → Dr Seuss's first book was rejected by 27 publishers.
- → Lucille Ball was once known as 'The Queen of B Movies' before she got her big break.
- → Sir James Dyson went through 5126 failed prototypes for his vacuum cleaner over 15 years. The 5127th prototype worked.
- → Stephen King's wife retrieved an early draft of *Carrie* from the bin, encouraging him to have another go.
- → Lady Gaga was dropped by her record label after three months.
- → Vivienne Westwood opened her legendary punk clothing store, Sex, at the age of 36 and launched her first runway show at 41.
- → *Mad Men* actors John Slattery and John Hamm were cast at 44 and 36 respectively.

The list of late bloomers goes on and on ... Paul Cezanne, Robert Frost, Charles Darwin, Claude Monet, Virginia Woolf, Anton Bruckner, Rickie Lambert, Kenneth Grahame, Emperor Claudius, Julia Child, Laura Ingalls Wilder, Martha Stewart, Albert Einstein, Alan Rickman, Sheryl Crow, Andrea Bocelli, Leonard Cohen ...

The way to success is paved with people who fell over, crawled on their knees, laid another stone in the path before them and got up again. The question is, are we prepared, at any age, to get down and crawl alongside them? Or will we let fear of it being 'too late' or feeling out of time stop us before we begin?

IT'S QUICKER TO DO SOMETHING ELSE

It's probably my job to tell you life isn't fair, but I figure you already know that. So instead, I'll tell you hope is precious, and you're right not to give up.

C.J. Redwine, *Defiance*

When we first started our 'My 15 Minutes' program, we were so excited about it we threw ourselves in 'boots and all' and made rapid progress in pulling everything together. After a few months of enjoyable 'slog', we reached a plateau where everything was running smoothly and we were experiencing a certain level of success.

That's when a weird thing happened. Instead of staying on the sharp upwards curve of achievement, taking the program higher and wider, we started getting all kinds of sideways ideas not related to the program. For other projects. Different approaches. Shiny new beginnings, each sparkling with fresh potential.

We found ourselves tempted to play out what George Leonard refers to as the 'master dabbler' pattern in his book, *Mastery: The keys to success and long-term fulfillment*. According to Leonard, a 'master' is someone who understands that progress is not as regular as the 'learning curve' we imagine. There are plateaus, dips and rises along the way. In those plateaus, a master will persist and keep practising (any new skill), even when it's hard or it seems they're getting nowhere. Dabblers, on the other hand, love new endeavours! They throw themselves into new sports, career opportunities and relationships with gusto. They love the rituals of getting started: the new equipment, timetables, branding, networks … The first spurt of progress is addictive! They can't wait for the next step, and also make rapid early progress.

Eventually, though, along comes the plateau. *Sigh*. Enthusiasm wanes. Lessons are missed. Thoughts creep in like, 'This really isn't for me …' And then something else catches the dabbler's eye.

We don't have to be 'masters' at everything we do. Mastery requires an enormous amount of dedication. There are some things we're all happy to dabble at, and variety can be wonderful. However, when you're striving for the thing that *does* matter to you, that you really do want to master, it helps to know to expect the plateaus. It helps to have a plan to persist through them. There's a need to practise, even when you feel you're not making progress. These are the times when you feel 'not enough' and struggle with comparisons against others further up the road. Once we burst through a plateau, there's another upwards curve towards higher competency and greater success that's worth pushing towards, no matter how late we're starting.

BUT I'M REALLY ON THE WRONG PATH

> To thine own self be true, and it must follow, as the night the day, thou canst not then be false to any man.
>
> William Shakespeare

Danica McKellar, who played Kevin Arnold's love interest Winnie Cooper in *The Wonder Years*, swept through social media in an inspiring video produced by NOVA on the 'secret life of scientists'.

'You're so recognized for this one role,' she said. 'And when that's over you start to wonder, "Who else would I be if I didn't have this?"'

She took a class in mathematics at UCLA and said she was afraid of it. She didn't know if she could do it. She thought 'doing well' belonged to someone who looked the part more than she did. After Danica scored at the top of her calculus class, above 163 people, her professor took her aside and let her know she had a gift and should pursue it. She became a calculus tutor, she co-authored a research paper and proved a new theorem. 'I discovered that I could be smart and capable and valuable for something that had nothing to do with Hollywood. This is me. And it felt great.'

Businesswoman Rebecca Derrington, founder of SourceBottle, encapsulated what so many of us have felt when we've trodden a certain path, only to realize it's the wrong one. We interviewed her and, speaking of her moment of realization, she said:

I decided I couldn't field one more legal enquiry, or jot down one more unit on a time sheet, or research one more legal issue … it was just killing me inside. I filled in that application form to go back to university and start the whole process all over again studying business and majoring in marketing and public relations. I was at the stage where you think you're done with your tertiary debts. You're starting to pay them off, not create new ones.

I couldn't stay a full-time student for very long. I had to fund a new career. And while I don't regret studying law and exercising that kind of intestinal fortitude, getting admitted and practicing for a brief period … I'm just glad it's in my past, and not in my future. I think it's helped shape who I am, and I think there was no way that I could stymy my passion for something else any longer. Not for one more second.

It's not something you can ignore. I remember sitting in a play. I was watching *The Mousetrap* in London — and I was sitting there thinking, 'How many more years would I need before I could retire … trying to justify my decision? At least 40 years … I just can't do it.' It was such a big thing to turn my back on, and to go back to waiting tables to fund a different degree. My parents were mortified! I still think they describe me as a lawyer first.

There was an expectation that if I had a chance to pursue a more serious career in a field like law, then that was expected of me. That expectation continued to seeing it right through to the end, past the admission — to make sure I really, really hated it before I decided I was going to do something else.

Rebecca's bold move out of her first career back through university and into her second is a choice that many people take, but many more dream of doing and don't, due to fear. It takes courage to admit that you've chosen something that isn't working for you, whether that's a decision in your personal or professional life. There can be a sense that some pride is at stake, you can have other people telling you what they expect, or what they would do. You can worry about accruing more debt or returning to a lower income — and those are genuine concerns.

At the end of the day, if you find yourself in the audience of a play, or watching TV, or on the sidelines of sport, and all you're thinking about is how miserable you are in your career or in another choice, it's time to do something about it. Not later, after this next little period of busyness passes. Not when you save more money or lose weight or when the kids are older. Now.

And what of Rebecca now? She completed her second degree and founded SourceBottle, which has grown to become a free global service that crowdsources expert sources for journalists, bloggers and reporters in the United States, Canada, the United Kingdom, Australia and New Zealand. We suspect she still thinks about work when she's in West End theatres … but in a good way.

HITTING ROCK BOTTOM

The best time to plant a tree is 20 years ago. The second best time is now.

Chinese proverb

Angela Raspass has a thriving business helping women from all over the world move into the next chapters of their professional lives in their forties and beyond. She lives in a beautiful part of Sydney with her husband and teenage children and she loves life.

Ten years ago, though, it was a very different story, one driven by a cycle of self-loathing, guilt and addiction. Sometimes when you think it's too late to change, you forfeit the bigger and more beautiful life that is available to you. And change is always possible. Here's Angela's story.

I used to hide it. It was scary. It was shameful. Now I see it as a point of inspiration: if I can get out of this, anyone can. I thought I was alone. I didn't know anyone who was battling it. I thought I was 'terminally unique'. I used to agonize, 'Why didn't I find this sooner?' I was 37. But now I see myself as one of the incredibly lucky ones.

I didn't identify as being an alcoholic. That was a guy on a park bench, in an overcoat, with a brown paper bag on a bench outside Central Station. It certainly wasn't me, out here in the northern suburbs, with a nice house and car and job and kids and husband and a bottle of bourbon hidden behind the sofa.

The way I dealt with pain was to numb it. When I first drank, those feelings of 'uncomfortability' and high sensitivity of not fitting in dissolved. Low self-esteem was soluble in alcohol. When you are in emotional pain and you find that thing that removes that pain, it's the most logical thing in the world to do it again. For a lot of years, it didn't have a visibly negative impact. In your teens and your twenties, everyone (you think) is having a few drinks. With 'kindsight', I can see that I wasn't drinking normally from the start. I was drinking for the effect — to feel comfortable in my own skin. I was a chameleon. I needed the loosening up of the alcohol to become the person you needed me to be. It made me more 'acceptable'. I found approval. And I'd do it again. And again. Until one day you wake up and you realize it's no longer a choice.

The last six months of my addiction was the worst time of my life. My children were seven and three. I'd tried health farms. I'd tried a controlled drinking program. I'd even imported subliminal hypnotherapy CDs and herbs from South America. I'd stay on the wagon for six or seven weeks, but when an emotional crisis hit, I had no way of dealing with it, so I resorted to the only mechanism I knew to relieve pain, and it was the numbing again. You don't grow, emotionally. I didn't have tools to deal with the stuff that hurt. I was drinking every day. I'd given up. I was deeply rooted in the most intense shame and the chances of asking for help were pretty low. I was drinking a bottle of vodka in a day.

There's a difference between surrendering and giving up. I realized I didn't have the answers. I'd fought it. I'd tried everything. And I just surrendered.

I remember there had been this one night. Everyone was asleep. I remember going into the bathroom and really looking at myself in the mirror: I was so filled with self-loathing, I could put on makeup without looking at myself. This night, I really looked into my eyes and there was such sadness that this was where I was at with my life. I knew I was worth so much more than the way I was treating myself, but I just couldn't connect the dots. There was that moment of utter desolation and pain that I saw, truly for the first time. And that's when I knew it just *had* to change. I surrendered. I said, 'I can't do it. I need help.' And that's when help arrived.

I began to hear the messages of possibility. I soaked it up like a sponge. I did all of the suggested things. I changed a lot of things. I did a twelve-step program. I took responsibility. There were a lot of things I had to do, if I wanted a different life.'

Ten years of sobriety later, the contrast in Angela's life couldn't be more marked.

I'm living from the inside out. My life is so completely different. The personal development and emotional maturity is huge. I embrace the idea that there's something bigger than me in the world. I recognize that I am worthy. I have a place in the world and I'm going to be looked after. I feel connected to purpose. I have a right to be here. I have a contribution to make. I don't have to prove anything. I consider myself 'first equal' in my life. I am

as important as everyone else — not more
or less. I read and meditate, walk and mix
with people who have a calm energy about
them. I am far more accepting of other
people and far less judgmental. I'm present
now. I absolutely believe in second chances
for people. I've been loved back to life.

Our greatest glory is not in never
failing, but in rising up every time we
fail.

Ralph Waldo Emerson

One afternoon we confided in each other about conversations each
of us had had with our respective sisters, Michele and Sarah, about
fearing that our marriages would never measure up to the 'golden'
relationships lived over many decades by our parents. We'd already
had conversations about how far short we felt our parenting fell
compared with what we both described as 'perfection' when thinking
of how our parents managed it. Thankfully, Emma's mum set the record
straight on that: 'You didn't see all the times I was so exhausted from
being a mum I'd stand in the shower, holding the top of the screen to
stop myself from falling over crying.'

We both feel privileged to have been raised by parents with 'once
in a lifetime' love. But along with that privilege comes a high ideal
standard. When you have parents who met and fell in love young, and
lived into their later years together, rarely exchanging cross words,
rarely arguing or seemingly even feeling irritated with each other —
parents whose love for each other always lit up the room, in sickness

and in health — it's hard not to compare your own performance in a relationship and rate it poorly.

One of our favourite movie quotes is from *Shadowlands*: 'Why love, if losing hurts so much? … The pain now is part of the happiness then. That's the deal.' Sadly, we're both now in the position of watching our parents in pain, which is made more intense because of the happiness of having had lives entwined since they were teenagers. Cancer steals life from the body; Alzheimer's steals it from the mind. Both diseases tear the hearts from the people who are left, who find super-human strength to see their partners through. It hurts to watch.

Love is messy. Even the fairytale kind. Sometimes it unravels before we have the chance to hold each other's hands in nursing homes. Divorce rips the rug from under us and scatters everything sideways. It feels like that even if we are the ones who do the ripping. It's a time when we question everything we know about ourselves, and wonder how we'll ever stagger to our feet again and move forward. It's being in a fire. And once that fire recedes and the ashes cease to glow hot red, the greenery starts sprouting again no matter what the outcome is, even if it means a very different kind of life.

Audrey:

Interestingly, for a life-long people pleaser I chose to politely ignore a number of well-meaning friends in their efforts to convince me that I should 'fight for my marriage'. I knew soon after my ex-husband, Warren, shared with me his feelings about our relationship that I would not kick and scream to convince him to stay. I wanted more than that for me and for him. In hindsight, I can see that it was a situation of either 'all in or all out'.

I'd been hurt before and experienced the end of a relationship, but this was a whole new experience. I could feel my chance of 'happily ever after with a couple of kids' being ripped from me. Initially, I felt I had few choices but of course I did. It just took a few days for that realization to kick in.

We sought relationship counselling, which helped enormously, but even in the very early days of the separation, I felt strongly the goal of the counselling for me was not about 'winning him back' — it was about me creating a path of my own, cobbling together strategies to learn from this relationship and move on. I chose to honour the many reasons we married in the first place, and I would never regret the years we spent together. Hating him at the end of our marriage simply because he was being honest with me about his feelings seemed wrong and ill-fitting for me and yet other people thought I should be less caring and understanding than I chose to be.

I quickly made the decision that I would be okay. I would get through this minefield of fresh, raw, heartbreaking change and would come out the other end of this still being me. I remember one day imagining I had a sticky note stuck on my forehead. On that note I had written two words: DIGNITY and INTEGRITY. Like it was yesterday, I recall telling myself, 'If you can get through all of this with these two things still intact, you'll be okay.' And that's what I did — and, thankfully, so did he. Warren and I didn't argue throughout our separation, or since. There were no acrimonious situations. No blaming. No spite. In fact, there were moments of lightness and humour even as we sold our home and the land upon which we had been planning to build our dream home.

In fairness, though, there were times I felt angry, bitter, resentful and full of sadness. I wanted to shout from the rooftops of the injustice of feeling as if I had no choice in my future. But those moments were the exception rather than the rule. When friends asked me how I was doing, I rarely felt the need to get into the blame-game and often wondered with amusement why other people felt so betrayed and indignant about the situation when I didn't.

Since we didn't have any children together, it would be easy to assume that we wouldn't need to keep in touch or be in each other's lives at all. I'm glad that's not the case. Each of us has married again and had children. Life has moved on in so many ways but even now, I'm pleased that Daf and I can call Warren and his wife, Rachael, our friends.

Fast forward a few years and life looked very different for me. I was living in the United Kingdom and loving my work and the life I'd created in London. Footloose and fancy-free. In 2002, none of my friends was keen to go on a sailing holiday with me, so I booked a solo two-week trip to Nidri, on the beautiful Greek island of Lefkas. I made some wonderful new friends and it was halfway through my stay that I met a quirky Welshman who was working for the yacht holiday company. Apparently opposites do attract. Everything about this situation seemed implausible but I had a strong feeling that this was right, and that he was right for me.

After two years of me travelling between Greece and London, daily phone calls and the challenges of being in a long-distance relationship, Daf moved to London and we embarked upon our second-time-round marriage, for both of us. We certainly had the fairytale start to our new life, getting married in a gorgeous castle in the heart of Scotland, with our closest family and friends. We announced at the wedding that we were expecting our first child and we couldn't have been happier.

Much as I loved living abroad, I always knew I'd return home and that raising kids in the United Kingdom wasn't something I wanted to do. Faced with that, Daf did then what he does so resolutely now — in so many aspects of our life as a couple and as a family — he supported me. And for that I will always be grateful. The following year, Daf was granted a visa to move to Australia with me just in time for Fin's birth. We moved our lives across the globe and while I was excited to be returning to my home town and my family, I knew that this had come at a cost to the family

Daf and I were creating, and particularly to him. He made an enormous sacrifice for me, for us. Leaving his parents, brothers and best friends behind was difficult for him then and has been over the years since, no more so than when losing his dad, Evan, and being so far away from his mum as she continued her fight with cancer.

Our life together now isn't perfect. Far from it. But it's real, and it's full of love and mutual respect. Somewhere along the way I realized that it wasn't important (or even helpful) to aspire to a relationship that matched the uniqueness of my parents'. We have our own uniqueness and it works for us.

Stalwart in his commitment to me and our sons, and his love for us all, Daf and this relationship were worth the wait.

Emma:

My daughters were flower girls when they were seven and nine and I helped them dress for the wedding at the bride's house. It was a hive of activity, with her parents, sister and best friend there too. I made cups of tea and stayed for photos, then waved them all off in the cars as they headed for the church. Then I went away for the weekend.

It was their dad's wedding. The bride — their step-mum, Helen — had invited me to her house that morning to help with the girls (and because she knew I'd want to see them dressed up like this for the first time). It was as unconventional as it was comfortable and in the years that followed we spent Christmas breakfasts in each other's houses so no one would miss the excitement.

People admire how amicable it has been, and that's been no accident. I've poured more energy and tears than I thought humanly possible into making our 'functional dysfunctional' family work. We've had our moments, of course, but for the most part have remained firmly focused on delivering to our daughters a low-stress relationship between their parents.

Helen and Matt have two little girls of their own now, and they moved to a city in another state when our two were eleven and nine. I got the call about the change in arrangements while I was on bedrest a few weeks into my pregnancy with my little boy, and it turned our lives completely upside down. Newly married, my husband and I flipped back to having the girls full-time just as they were about to hit high school. I regarded the unexpected extra time with them as precious, though the separation broke their hearts.

Sometimes my ex-husband's children have video calls with our little boy. None of them has quite pieced together in their minds how it is that the three of them share some older sisters, whom they mutually adore. And those sisters now have an older step-sister and step-brother, too — my husband's children from his first marriage. My step-children's mum and I sometimes have lunch and catch up on how all the children are going. She sends me articles that might be useful for the girls, we talk about raising older children and about ageing parents and how we juggle it all.

My husband, Jeff, has seen my children through some tough years, emotionally. Parenting teenagers of your own is a big deal. Step-parenting someone else's teenagers, full-time, probably deserves some kind of award! He has worked so hard for me and my daughters. And he's done endless grocery runs and cooked endless healthy dinners (sometimes to a mixed reception). He's stood beside me as I've helped them navigate some really tough experiences. He's ignored the drama as they've flapped about school assignments or work shifts. He's given us space as they've cried about broken hearts or 'friend problems' or about missing their dad. He's put up with their mess, their moods and their music but, perhaps most notably, he's sacrificed more than one brilliant career opportunity because a move interstate would not have been best for one of my girls at the time.

Our little boy, Sebastian, cemented our 'Brady Bunch' when he came along in 2010. With an age range of the children in our family of 21 years, life is a whirlwind of dinosaurs and Thomas trains, of teen spirit and young adults exploring early careers, serious relationships and the world, in a way that makes my heart sing and race and thud to a stop, on occasion. I've never felt more alive.

These are all the different ways the greenery has grown from the ashes after one story or another has ended. This is what happens because it's never too late to start a new chapter. It's never too late in any aspect of your life. A healthier way of living, new friendships and relationships, new careers or businesses, new hobbies or interests. These changes happen when we do as Angela did, and place ourselves as 'first equal' in our lives. And starting new things need not seem overwhelming if tackled one small step at a time.

EXPERIMENT 29:
YOUR HEALTH AND WELLBEING
JUST THE NEXT STEP

Whether it's managing stress more proactively, losing weight, getting fit or carving better boundaries between work and home, it's never too late to make big changes in your health and wellbeing. These can often seem overwhelming, which is why focusing on *just* the next step, and not the big picture, can really help.

Choose to do one of the following.

For better management of mental health: **Turn off all your phones and other gadgets — create a 'no pinging' zone. Lie down on the floor (or on a yoga mat if you have one), with your knees up and feet flat on the floor. Widen your elbows to the sides, with your hands resting gently on your abdomen. You may like to rest your head on a couple of books to create alignment with your spine (not a cushion, as this still involves some muscle work in your neck). Now close your eyes and breathe. Let thoughts simply come and go. Stay there for 15 minutes.**

For better management of physical health: **Go for a 15-minute walk or do 15 minutes of physical activity (with permission from your doctor, of course).**

↑ **15 MINUTE MAGIC** →

EXPERIMENT 30: YOUR RELATIONSHIPS HO'OPONOPONO

Ho'oponopono is a Hawaiian affirmation or prayer meaning to 'make right'. It is a practice of accepting responsibility and creating healing in ourselves and our relationships in order to let go and move on. As sceptical as you may feel about the idea of a simple mantra giving us the capacity to heal emotionally, consider the alternative: that we're already chanting 'mantras' of a very different and damaging kind. The type that swirl in our minds when we hold a grudge, withhold forgiveness or continue to let past wrongs hold us captive.

It's never too late to let these things go and to release ourselves from feelings of upset, bitterness or regret. It's liberating when we do.

Find a quiet time to pause and reflect on a situation that has been holding you captive for too long. As you think about the situation, or the person, recite several times the Ho'oponopono:

**I'm sorry
Please forgive me
I love you
Thank you.**

Do this even if it seems to jolt with the way you feel at first. This is about self-forgiveness, self-love and gratitude as much as it is about forgiving others. It is a gift to yourself, and through you, a gift to the world around you.

EXPERIMENT 31:
YOUR CAREER AND BUSINESS
PICK YOUR PATH

Throughout this book, there has been a mix of tasks relating to facets of your life. Some have been practical 'hands-on' activities to help you become more organized or productive, others focused on shifting your mindset related to career growth, communication, relationships and performance. Tom Freston, co-founder and former chair and CEO of MTV, shared this view: 'A career path is rarely a path at all. A more interesting life is usually a more crooked, winding path of missteps, luck and vigorous work. It is almost always a clumsy balance between the things you try to make happen and the things that happen to you.'

In the context of your career (or business, if you're self-employed), we have a blunt question for you: Are you on the right path? Yes or no?

This can be a grey area, but what is your gut response?

If your answer to our question is yes: that's good! Spend 15 minutes mind-mapping a rough plan for 'what next?' along your current path. What gaps need to be filled? What is the *first* next step?

If your answer is no: that's good too! Spend 15 minutes mind-mapping a series of options, questions to ask and people to speak to. What is the *first* next step?

That's okay for you but ...

I'm 30. I'm 40. I'm 50. I'm 60.

It doesn't matter if we don't have it all worked out at 30, 40 or even 60. It really doesn't. Now is the right time to decide your first next step.

EXPERIMENT 32: YOUR FINANCES
STUFF

In most situations in our lives, it's never too late to start doing the things which bring more joy, fun, connection, personal growth and improved wellbeing.

How often do you hear yourself saying, 'We don't have the money for that right now' or 'We'll do that once we've bought the new [insert material 'stuff']'? You'd love to spend more time doing fun things with family and friends, but you're not sure how to free up the money to do it. The answer might be simpler than you think.

Spend more money 'doing stuff' than 'on stuff'.

Think about the money you spend in a typical month shopping at stores, eating in restaurants and ordering from fast-food outlets. How much of that is what you would consider essential spending? Be honest with yourself. It's likely there's a gap between truly necessary expenses and what you're actually spending in retail outlets. The uncomfortable reality is that this extra spending isn't going toward things you'll remember years from now — often it is discretionary expenditure being put into 'stuff'. Instantly gratifying, yet often quickly forgotten, stuff.

Now consider redirecting some of your monthly budget to family activities, memorable day trips or holidays — imagine the difference that could make in your life. Eliminating even $10 from your day-to-day spending frees up $3650 this year for experiencing more of those memory-making moments.

Spend a few minutes now creating a financial goal that inspires you. Be specific about setting your sights on a particular target, such as a holiday in a tropical resort or a few weekend mini-breaks to spots you love or would love to visit.

EXPERIMENT 33: YOUR PERSONAL GROWTH
STRIKE A POSE

Scientists have found direct links between our physiology and emotions. Smiling has been found to reduce stress and increase wellbeing, and Harvard researcher Amy J.C. Cuddy was one of the researchers who conducted a 2010 experiment into the impact of 'power poses' on confidence.

When participants in the study took just 2 minutes to stand confidently — in a tall, expansive posture, like the classic 'superhero' pose with their chins up and arms strong beside them — they not only reported feeling stronger and took more risks as part of the experiment, but their measurable testosterone levels increased and the stress hormone, cortisol, dropped. Standing in a 'power pose' literally gave them an extra surge of power and a sense of wellbeing.

'The poses we used in the experiment are strongly associated across the animal kingdom with high and low dominance for very straightforward evolutionary reasons,' Dr Cuddy explained in a *Harvard Business School* article. 'Either you want to be big because you're in charge, or you want to close in and hide your vital organs because you're not in charge.' The technique can be used ahead of situations in which we typically feel nervous, like job interviews or key presentations.

Suspend disbelief and spend some time standing in a 'power pose' — tall, chin up, strong arms. Really get 'out of your head' and 'into your body' and let your subconscious mind do its stuff.

Observe how you feel afterwards, and over the course of the next few days (or weeks) aim for fifteen powerful moments when you shift your body or emotions and feel the positive benefits of being mindful of your physicality.

Mindfully acknowledge those times when you're required to step up and do something nerve-wracking.

15 MINUTE MAGIC

EXPERIMENT 34: YOUR HOME
PAY IT FORWARD

A number of the activities in this book and in our 90-day program rely upon being able to enjoy the outdoors. People often report to us in our Facebook group how lovely it is to lie on the ground under a tree, looking up, and to experience some time either alone or with others, outside. Now it's time to give back, and ensure this opportunity is available for future generations, while having some fun!

Take 15 minutes to plant a tree. It really doesn't matter what type of tree, its age or where you plant it — this is about paying it forward for the greater good. If you live some distance from the nearest nursery, this challenge may take slightly more than 15 minutes but will be worth it. Emma's dad, who is 84, suggested this 15-minute challenge. He is acutely aware of taking opportunities like this now, for the people who will come after us.

We'd love to see a photo of your tree on social media. Use the hashtag #Idonthavetimebook #plantatree

EXPERIMENT 35: YOUR FUN AND RECREATION
NAME YOUR ADVENTURES

During those long, lonely months in hospital when Emma's daughter's friend had cancer, the girls would sit on the bed and plan a list of the 'mini-adventures' they'd have when she was finally released. They knew there were some limitations. Her immune system was shot, and she couldn't be in crowded places or near sick people. They were young and didn't have money to spend, so they had to be imaginative. It wasn't until years later that they admitted one of the adventures they'd accomplished was to sneak in and have a swim in the pool at a five-star hotel they weren't staying at! Note: we're not advocating trespass in this task!

We can become so entangled in our own comfort zones that we forget how exhilarating it can be to step out of them. We want you to plan a series of adventures with a focus on stretching yourself out of your comfort zone and into play, fun and new experiences. No matter what you choose, make it something that you normally wouldn't do. Keep it safe and legal, but make it a little bit scary! Every small step we take into unknown territory helps us grow.

This activity seems so simple (and it can be) but we know you'll love it — especially when you look back on what you've achieved in 12 months' time. We want you to spend 15 minutes deciding on twelve mini-adventures (or fun challenges) you are going to commit to over the next year.

Start by writing down at least twelve activities you'd like to try, places you'd like to visit or experiences you'd like to enjoy. Jot down all of the things about which you've ever thought, 'One day, I'll do that (or go there)'. Then, make a commitment to yourself to start planning for these fun challenges, each and every month.

These mini-adventures don't need to be expensive or difficult; they can be free and right on your doorstep. Have you tried geocaching in your local area, or borrowing a skateboard or scooter and braving the twists and turns of a skate park with the neighbourhood kids? (Audrey did this recently, and felt fifteen again!) If it's been a while, dust off your bike, rollerblades or hiking boots and get out there into the great outdoors. Whatever it is, have fun and enjoy the gift of living that you're giving to yourself!

FINAL THOUGHTS

We invested six months in writing this book, and we could easily have invested another six. We could have added to it and tweaked it for another two years, or more. We could shove it in a drawer and come back to it in a decade — and that's what lots of writers do, because we're grappling with the knowledge that what we write will never be perfect. It's in our best interests, though, and in yours, that we leave our efforts here and move on. There are other things we want to accomplish in our careers. Other programs we want to develop. Other books we want to write.

There's a knack to knowing when to stop. The trick is in being able to accept that your work could always be improved upon, but *your time isn't always best spent improving upon it*. And part of that is taking a deep breath and preparing yourself for what is coming next.

Emma:

A few years ago I was asked to go on a breakfast TV show after a rant I'd written about the 'mummy wars' was published in a tabloid newspaper.

'Hello, this is Leah,' a woman had said on the phone, while I was breastfeeding my baby son. 'Would you be interested in appearing live in our studios tomorrow morning at 7.40 a.m.?'

Gaaaahh! No hair cut in six months! The camera adds 10 pounds! I've put on 20 kilos!

'In the next 10 minutes, can you email me your top five tips, and the five biggest mistakes women make when balancing work and family?' Leah had said.

Eek! Sebastian needed a bottle, Sophie had ballet and the ex-in-laws were on their way over ...

'The studio is at the Senate entrance to Parliament House. Do you know it?'

Not as such ...

'Great! If you have any questions, I start work at 4 a.m. Bye!'

She hung up and it was time to collect my wits. In what transpired to be a mistake as far as collecting my wits went, I immediately took to Facebook to ask for advice. Sixty-seven comments later, I'd learned that I had to wear block colours, perhaps a black top with a scarf, or a black dress and, as it was in the Canberra studio, the shoot would only involve my top half, so I should focus on that and not worry so much about pants.

Well. I'd *wear* pants, obviously, but it didn't matter if they didn't fit or match.

A mental inventory of my black tops revealed that the only one that wasn't faded or too tight was a cheap black pyjama top I'd bought to wear in the hospital after the baby was born. I'd recently worn it in the gold class movie theatre and nobody had noticed. Although it was pitch dark. I explained this on Facebook.

'I dare you to wear your PJs on national television!' a friend quipped.

I would! Yes.

Except I was wearing the top *now* — at 4 p.m. the night before the 7 a.m. interview. And it was now drenched in infant formula. Would it dry in time?

Julia Gillard was the Australian Prime Minister at the time. Did she go through this anguish before TV appearances? She never seemed to be photographed in her pyjamas. She seemed to wear white jackets. Nobody said anything about white! They all said black. It's all right for her! Wasn't her partner a hairdresser? Mine is a military historian ...

I set about writing my top five tips. Interchangeable pyjamas and work gear was a good one. Maybe I could tell mums to sleep in what they'll wear the next day, like kids do before an early start.

'Wear a baby on your nipple,' a male friend suggested. What? Oh, yes, the story was about feeding babies and returning to work. So — go for authenticity, you think? Should I listen to him? The man owns a second-hand book shop and was about as qualified as my husband to provide fashion advice.

In any case, Seb hadn't latched on once in five months. It's hard enough feeding in a shopping centre, let alone in front of cameras and a spotlight and hundreds of thousands of viewers, while you attempt to string together a coherent sentence.

'Plan B,' he suggested, channeling Bernard from *Black Books*, 'is a hip flask of whisky.'

Right. PJs and a hip flask. Pants optional. Is that tip number two?

By this stage I'd bought into my own hysteria and was shaking in my boots. *Shoes!* Did I have any? Surely I must!

Oh, it's okay. Feet won't be on screen. Focus on hair, focus on hair ...

My daughter had recently been playing with my hair, and said, 'Did you know you have forty-nine grey hairs just in this portion of your head alone?' That had been weeks before! Who knew how many I had now if you tallied up the entire head. It was too late for an appointment. Should I attempt dyeing it myself? I'd only done that once before and it had been an unmitigated disaster.

'You remind me of Kellie,' the same daughter said.

Who?

'You know. She's one of the contestants on *The Biggest Loser* ...'

Whaaaat?

'You have similar hair.'

Oh, the relief!

The phone rang again.

'It's Leah, here, from Channel Nine. Look, I'm terribly sorry to do this to you,' Leah said, 'but there's been a celebrity break-up. We're going to have to run that story instead of yours.'

The relief!

Fast forward a few years and we'd barely popped the champagne after hearing about our publishing deal for this book, when the negative mindset gremlins started to creep in. When we have a book, we'll need to do media interviews. Radio, we can handle. But what if we're asked to go on the morning TV shows? *Gah!* Here we go again ...

At times like this, which involve quite a big step up from what you're used to, there's often a tiny voice that says, 'It would be easier if this didn't happen.' Even when we're unsatisfied in our comfort zones, even when we want something *very much*, we can prefer to feel protected and safe. There's comfort in cancelled plans, if those plans meant some kind of 'stretch'. Our fears aren't always around 'What if I fail?' Sometimes they're about what might change if we succeed, about the new demands that might be placed upon us. We might need to go on TV. We might need to take the lead on a presentation that scares us. Our relationships with co-workers or friends might change. *What will my partner think? Will my friends still like me? Will people resent me?* And the big one: *Will I be able to handle the next steps?*

Unashamed misfits unite!

'I wasn't born a world champion,' explained seven-time world champion surfer, Layne Beachley, when we spoke to her.

I was the only girl in the water and I started to encroach on the northern end of the beach where I started to get harassed, intimidated, threatened, kicked out of the water: you're a girl, you're not allowed out here. And I broke down those barriers because I wanted something so desperately. I was so passionate about becoming the best in the world at something that I wasn't going to allow some dream-thief out there who didn't have the courage and the conviction to set a goal, let alone the determination to achieve it, tell me that I'm not capable of doing something.

Author Alexandra Robbins has written a book called *The Geeks Shall Inherit the Earth: Popularity, Quirk Theory and why outsiders thrive after high school*, in which she describes her Quirk Theory. She believes that the skills and idiosyncrasies that lead us to feel excluded or ignored in high school are the same traits that earn us respect, admiration and success in adult life. 'Nothing is more unnerving to the truly conventional,' says Robbins, 'than the unashamed misfit.'

The life you want might not be conventional. It might not be shaped the way your family wants it shaped. Your friends might do a double-take when they hear your plans. It might not work, at first. But we're not here to live the lives others want. We're not here to hide our lights. We're here to leave our legacies, and legacies aren't left by people whose time is sucked away by perfection. They're not left by people who struggle alone or spend all their time doing others' bidding. They're not left by people scared to get it wrong.

Legacies are left by people who understand that the legacy matters most. They're left by people who spend their lives running towards what they want, and not away from what they don't want. They're left by people who see an obstacle and go around, over, under or through. They're left by people who can't get over that obstacle alone, so they enlist someone else's help.

Legacies are left by people who know with all of their being that there is *exactly* enough time for all the important things in life.

CHOOSE HEALTH. CHOOSE RELATIONSHIPS. CHOOSE WHAT MAKES YOUR SOUL SING.

—

EDUCATE THE PEOPLE AROUND YOU ABOUT WHAT YOU WILL AND WON'T DO. THE 'DITCH THIS' LIST DETERMINES THE QUALITY OF YOUR LIFE.

—

PUT DOWN THE MOP AND BUCKET. YOU ARE NOT THERE TO CLEAN UP EVERYONE ELSE'S MESS AT WORK, AT HOME AND IN YOUR TRIBE.

—

YOU ARE NOT THERE TO SWOOP ON EVERY CRY FOR HELP YOU HEAR AND EVERY EMERGENCY RESULTING FROM OTHERS' POOR PLANNING. BEING BRILLIANT AT PUTTING YOURSELF LAST ISN'T BEING LIKED, IT'S BEING TAKEN FOR GRANTED.

FUEL YOUR BODY AND MIND WITH THE THINGS THAT MAKE YOU STRONG.

FIT THE OXYGEN MASK TO YOURSELF FIRST,

AND BE CLEAR-HEADED TO HELP THOSE WHO MATTER MOST TO YOU.

—

LET GO OF OTHER PEOPLE'S DRAMA.

LET THEM FIND THEIR OWN OXYGEN AND THEIR OWN FEET TO STAND ON.

—

LET GO OF 'MARTYR', 'EXCUSES' AND 'PERFECT'.
LET GO OF 'NOBODY DOES THIS AS WELL AS I DO'.
LET GO OF 'I'LL DO IT LATER', 'IT'S TOO LATE' AND 'THERE'S NO WAY OUT'.
LET GO OF EYEING UP OTHER PEOPLE'S GREENER GRASS.
DROP 'SORRY' FROM THE BEGINNING OF EVERY SECOND SENTENCE.

ROAR 'NO'

QUIT RUNNING FROM WHAT YOU DON'T WANT.
STOP CLIMBING INTO BED WONDERING WHERE THE DAY WENT.

DIRECT YOUR DAY WITH VISION, BOUNDARIES AND ASSERTIVENESS.

LIVE THE LIFE YOU WANT FOR ANY CHILDREN IN YOUR LIFE.

TELL YOURSELF WHAT YOU WOULD WHISPER IN THEIR EARS:

You do have time...

EPILOGUE

While we were editing this book, the fabric was ripped from Emma's universe with the unexpected loss of her husband and soulmate, Jeff, from a heart attack.

When you lose the love of your life, it can bring you to your knees. It can completely destroy you. Or it can bring you to your feet.

When we interviewed Rebecca Sparrow for our '15 Minutes That Changed My Life' speaker series she told us about losing her baby daughter, Georgie. 'Somehow, Georgie was going to turn the light up in my life, not down,' Bec had said.

Emerging from the first few weeks of shock and devastation, Emma decided to do one life-affirming thing, no matter how small, every day — beginning with rearranging the flowers people had sent into beautiful bouquets and delivering them to a hospital with her children.

We also thought about the words we'd written in this book. Did this shattering tragedy change anything? Did it alter our perspective on life?

Yes, it did.

Jeff's loss is turning up the light in our lives, not down. We want to be better people. We want to do more. Experience more. *Live* more.

We're more committed than ever to the ideas we've presented in this book. We want to procrastinate less, focus more sharply, reach higher and further than we ever have without a backwards glance at our insecurities and fears, because life is short. Life is precious.

The time we have is a gift. Take it and turn up the light.

ACKNOWLEDGMENTS

As business partners, co-conspirators and besties, we thank our lucky stars for the opportunity to work together. Our thanks go to …

Our publisher, Anouska, who asked if we'd thought about writing a book together; thank you for planting the idea and championing it along the way.

Gareth, founder of Exisle Publishing, thanks for taking a chance on us.

Karen, our editor, thank you for your brilliant expertise in shaping our words.

Tracey, you captured our vision beautifully in the book's design.

Our wonderful 'My 15 Minutes' community, our gratitude for your trust and encouragement. Without you, this book wouldn't exist.

Our early readers, Barbara, Sarah, Michele, Barrie and Sandra, your enthusiasm buoyed our spirits and kept us writing.

FROM AUDREY

I'm a firm believer that inspiration, and indeed love, is all around, and I'm blessed that I don't need to look far for either. My family inspires me every day with their quirkiness, humour and strength. Their love is my life-force — wherever they are is my 'happy place'.

Daf, thank you for your patience, for all the times you believed in me and my dreams when my belief was wavering, and for being right beside me through everything. My love and gratitude, always, *cariad bach.*

Finlay and Will, you fill me up — with love, joy, laughter and pride, and so much more. Always be you.

My mum and dad, thank you for always being there for me and teaching me what really matters in life. My love and gratitude is more than I could put into words.

My sister and nephew, Michele and Alexander, thank you for everything! I could not ask for a more amazing sister.

My friends, far and near, thank you for your love, support and encouragement through all the good and not-so-good times.

My clients, you are the best and you know who you are! Thanks so much for putting your trust in me.

FROM EMMA

Sal, Alison, Julie and Nikki, your friendly 'nagging' on weekly word counts was crucial to this book's existence. Your friendship is crucial to mine.

Ali, Al and Lyndal, thank you for everything since we were twelve. Everything.

My parents and sister, Sarah, brother-in-law, Paul and nieces Abbey and Lucy, your love means the world to me.

Victoria and Duncan, Jake and Meg, thank you for your consistent love and support. You will always have mine.

Hannah and Sophie, you're the inspiration for my work and the legacy I want to leave. I'm incredibly proud of the resilient, passionate young women you're becoming.

Sebastian, my darling boy. This book was written in the last few months of Daddy's life. When you read it one day, know how precious time was to us, and how dearly we've loved the time we had together, particularly since you came along.

And to Jeff ... your belief in me, your unwavering support and the love you showed me until your dying day will live on in every word I ever write.

APPENDIX:

IF YOU THOUGHT IT WAS JUST YOU ...

Listed below are even more of the many and varied beliefs people hold about themselves which they've shared with us during our workshops:

→ I compare myself to other personalities and people I don't know well.

→ Someone else can do my job better than I can.

→ I can't format documents as well and as quickly as my colleagues. I always fail.

→ Others know more than me.

→ I don't want to get my colleagues to read my work because it will be poor quality compared with theirs.

→ I'm not a 'real' executive because I'm new to the role.

→ I am not successful enough.

→ I'm not applying for board roles, even though it's what I want to do, because I don't have enough experience.

→ I'm afraid of taking on higher responsibilities because I'm scared I don't know what I'm doing.

→ I do not deserve my job.

→ I have to do more and be more to earn my level/promotion.

→ I can't email/phone that executive because I'm not important enough.

→ Don't they realize I haven't done this particular task before?

→ I didn't want to apply for the job that I got (and didn't think I would get it).

- → I don't have the depth of knowledge I need.
- → I'm not smart, intelligent, skilled or confident enough to have the job I've got.
- → I'm going to be overestimated.
- → I'm not as effective at my job as I could be.
- → I'm not as good as others think I am.
- → I'm not liked or respected because I'm changing the way things have always been done.
- → I won't start a business or apply for managing positions because of fear of failing.
- → I have a fear of promotion because of my fear of failure/ being judged, and fear of not being there for my children and elderly parents. I fear I'm not good enough.
- → I can't volunteer for that project. It will probably be too hard and I'll fail.
- → I can't apply for that job because I'm terrible at interviews.
- → I worry about talking to that executive at work in case I say the wrong thing.
- → I hate doing presentations because I get so nervous.
- → My boss is such a perfectionist that it doesn't matter how good my work is, I know she'll change it. I continually second-guess my ability.
- → I'm afraid that if I push for a promotion and I'm successful, I'll end up not being able to do the job.
- → I'm afraid that if I write a draft report my boss will hate what I've done and I'll feel stupid.
- → I hold back in meetings and socially in case I sound stupid or say something wrong.
- → I fear making a bad presentation and looking unprofessional.
- → If I speak up at work I might lose my job (and not be able to pay my mortgage).
- → If I don't get the job I'm going for, people will think I'm not good enough.
- → I have a fear of writing minutes, knowing they will be reviewed and re-written.

→ I fear public speaking in case I am judged.

→ I'm afraid of starting a university degree in case I fail.

→ I fear falling in love again in case I get hurt.

→ I'm never going to pass this.

→ I am scared to leave the secure bubble of my current workplace.

→ I am not worthy!

→ I am not good enough.

→ I hold myself back. I doubt myself even when people tell me positive things that *deep down* I know to be true.

→ I don't know what I'm doing, and without my team I would not be very good.

→ If I leave, I will not have anything I'm good at.

→ I can't spend time with family because I'm too busy with work.

→ How am I going to get this project done by the due date?

→ Being a single mum makes me push myself harder and I'm overwhelmed.

→ I have a fear of taking on more work, then not being able to finish it.

→ I fear that I'll crack under pressure and then 'drop the bundle'.

→ This seems too hard or so unachievable I can't even try.

→ I'm far too overwhelmed to be a good leader.

→ I feel guilty and take on the ownership of issues that are not mine and/or I cannot control.

→ I'm a very bad mother by not spending enough time with my children.

→ I don't think I can do something when I haven't done it before.

→ I'm scared to take charge of situations in case I make a mistake.

→ I can't send an email without carefully checking everything is correct.

→ I take too long to ensure reports are word perfect when they probably don't need to be.

- → People will misinterpret this, so I have to go over it (in a loop).
- → I fail to work per prioritization because it all needs to get done.
- → I want to do it all at once, and right.
- → Higher priorities always come along and I need to get them done first.
- → I don't have time to clean the house because I have to spend time with my family.
- → I don't have time to do my course or clean because of being a single mum.
- → I have a fear of forgetting to do things (therefore I do the easy things first).
- → Now that I've passed, how will I actually pull this off and write for clients?
- → This could mean exposure or attention. I don't like being in the spotlight.
- → I fear getting more challenging work, leaving less time for my family.
- → People expect even more of me after I do well.
- → People will notice me more and talk about me if I succeed.
- → I don't know what's going to happen if this works. I'm scared of the unknown!

REFERENCES

INTRODUCTION

Carle, E. 1987, *The Very Hungry Caterpillar*, New York: Philomel Books.

Fielding, H. 1998, *Bridget Jones's Diary*, New York: Viking.

Gleick, J. 1999, *Faster: The acceleration of just about everything*, New York: Pantheon Books.

Grey, E. 2005, *Wits' End Before Breakfast! Confessions of a working mum*, Amazon.

Mackay, H. 2013, *The Good Life: What makes a life worth living?*, Sydney: Pan Macmillan.

Roosevelt, E. 2011, *You Learn by Living: Eleven keys for a more fulfilling life*, New York: Harper Perennial.

Salmansohn, K. 2007, *The Bounce Back Book: How to thrive in the face of adversity, setbacks, and losses*, New York: Workman Pub. Co., Inc.

Sings, M. 2015, *Selp-helf*, New York: Simon & Schuster.

Online

Grey, E. and Thomas, A. 2013, 'My 15 Minutes', available at: www.my15minutes.com.au

Manson, M. 2013, 'Stop trying to be happy', Mark Manson, available at: www.markmanson.net/stop-trying-to-be-happy

Thorne, C. 2016, 'Routine cartoon #523', Everyday People Cartoons, available at: www.everydaypeoplecartoons.com/cartoon/523

MINDSET GREMLIN 1

Angelou, M. 1994, *Wouldn't Take Nothing for My Journey Now*, (2nd ed.), New York: Bantam.

Grey, E. 2014, *Unrequited: Girl meets boy band*, Cork: BookBaby.

Hendricks, G. 2009, *The Big Leap: Conquer your hidden fear and take life to the next level*, New York: HarperCollins.

Holzapfel, K. 2016, *Selfless: A social worker's own story of trauma and recovery*, Canberra: Collaborative Publications.

Parkinson, C. 1958, *Parkinson's Law*, London: J. Murray.

Young, V. 2011, *The Secret Thoughts of Successful Women*, New York: Crown Business.

ONLINE

Grey, E. and Thomas, A. 2014, 'My 15 Minutes Speaker Series: The 15 Minutes That Changed My Life', My 15 Minutes Presents, available at: www.my15minutespresents.com

Haushofer, J. 2016, 'Johannes Haushofer CV of failures', available at: www.princeton.edu/haushofer

Humans of New York 2010, 'Humans of New York', available at: www.humansofnewyork.com

McGill University, 2016, 'The neuroscience of musical chills', available at: www.mcgill.ca/newsroom/channels/news/musical-chills-why-they-give-us-thrills-170538

Raspass, A. 2015, 'Have you lost your anchor?' available at: www.angelaraspass.com/have-you-lost-your-anchor

Voytek, B. 2011, 'Career ... advice?' Oscillatory Thoughts: Thoughts of a neuroscientist, available at: www.blog.ketyov.com/2011/08/career-advice.html.

VIDEO

Ira Glass on The Art of Storytelling, 2009, Minneapolis, MN: PRI Public Radio International.

MINDSET GREMLIN 2

Fox, M. 2010, *A Funny Thing Happened on the Way to the Future: Twists and turns and lessons learned*, New York: Hyperion.

Freeman, E. 2011, *Grace for the Good Girl: Letting go of the try-hard life*, Grand Rapids: Fleming H. Revell Company.

Hay, L. 1984, *You Can Heal Your Life*, Santa Monica: Hay House.

Marson, J. 2013, *The Curse of Lovely*, London: Piatkus.

ONLINE

Brown, B. 2008, 'Dedicated to Jen on her birthday', available at: www.brenebrown.com/2008/10/06/2008106dedicated-to-jen-on-her-birthday-html/

Chierchia, S. 2016, 'Sylvia Chierchia — financial coach', available at: www.sylviachierchia.com

MINDSET GREMLIN 3

Adams, D. 2002, *The Salmon of Doubt*, New York: Harmony Books.

Chapman, G. 1995, *The Five Love Languages*, Chicago: Northfield Publishing.

Crook, C. 2015, *The Joy of Missing Out: Finding balance in a wired world*, Gabriola Island: New Society Publisher.

Freeth, L. 2014, *Midget Gems: An autobiography*, Adelaide: Sunshine Press.

Jeffers, S. 2007, *Feel the Fear and Do It Anyway*, London: Vermilion.

Lamott, A. 1995, *Bird by Bird: Some instructions on writing and life*, New York: Anchor.

McGraw, K. and Fiala, J. 1982, 'Undermining the Zeigarnik effect: Another hidden cost of reward', *Journal of Personality*, 50: 58–66. doi: 10.1111/j.1467-6494.1982.tb00745.x, 50(1).

Miller, D. 2009, *The Butterfly Effect: A new approach to raising happy, confident teen girls*, North Sydney: Random House Australia.

Wiseman, L. 2004, *The Luck Factor: The scientific study of the lucky mind*, London: Arrow.

ONLINE

Brown, B. 2014, 'Why goofing off is really good for you', *Huffington Post*, available at: www.huffingtonpost.com/2014/02/03/brene-brown-importance-of-play_n_4675625.html

Clear, J. 2014, 'How the "Seinfeld Strategy" can help you stop procrastinating', *Entrepreneur*, available at: www.entrepreneur.com/article/231023

Swanson, A. 2016, 'The real reasons you procrastinate — and how to stop', *Washington Post*, available at: www.washingtonpost.com/news/wonk/wp/2016/04/27/why-you-cant-help-read-this-article-about-procrastination-instead-of-doing-your-job/

Urban, T. 2014, 'Why procrastinators procrastinate', *Huffington Post*, available at: www.huffingtonpost.com/wait-but-why/why-procrastinators-procrastinate_b_4369887.html

MINDSET GREMLIN 4

Brown, B. 2010, *The Gifts of Imperfection: Let go of who you think you're supposed to be and embrace who you are*, Center City: Hazelden.

Grout, P. 2013, *E-Squared: Nine do-it-yourself experiments that prove your thoughts create your reality*, Carlsbad: Hay House Insights.

Hopper, G. 1984, Commencement Address, Ohio State University.

McGregor, C. 2013, 'From Malcolm to Cate: My transformation', *Australian Women's Weekly*.

McGregor, M. 2012, *An Indian Summer of Cricket*, Griffith: Barrallier Books Pty Ltd.

ONLINE

LaMaitre, L. 2016, 'Childless: The grief of disappointment', Her Canberra, available at: www.hercanberra.com.au/cplife/childless-the-grief-of-disappointment/

Nightingale, E. 2016, 'The fog of worry (only 8% of worries are worth it)', Nightingale-Conant, available at: www.nightingale.com/articles/the-fog-of-worry-only-8-of-worries-are-worth-it/

MINDSET GREMLIN 5

Freston, T. 2007, Commencement Speech, Emerson College.

Leonard, G. 1991, *Mastery: The keys to success and long-term fulfillment*, New York: Plume.

Redwine, C. 2012, *Defiance*, New York: Balzer + Bray.

ONLINE

Derrington, R. 2009, SourceBottle, available at: www.sourcebottle.com.au

Hanna, J. 2010, 'Power posing: Fake it until you make it', HBS Working Knowledge, available at: www.hbswk.hbs.edu/item/power-posing-fake-it-until-you-make-it

The Complete Guide to the Alexander Technique. available at: www.alexandertechnique.com/constructiverest/

VIDEO

NOVA's Secret Life of Scientists and Engineers, 2016, 'Danica McKellar: Are you the girl from *The Wonder Years*?', available at: www.youtu.be/9KLMhhqCsbU

FINAL THOUGHTS

Robbins, A. 2011, *The Geeks Shall Inherit the Earth: Popularity, Quirk Theory, and why outsiders thrive after high school*, New York: Hyperion.

INDEX

A

Adams, Douglas 104
addiction, recovering from 163–7
adventures 180–1
alcoholism, recovering from 163–7
Andreas, Brian 3
Angelou, Maya 59, 64
approval, seeking 77–82
Astaire, Fred 157
Audrey
  bra incident 11–13
  eulogy for father 108–9
  father's sporting events 136–7
  imposter syndrome 55–6
  lack of confidence 26–30
  list of failures 49
  move to London 129–30
  personal relationships 168–71
  pleasing others 78–80
  regaining self-belief 56
Ayivor, Israelmore 51

B

'badge of honour' busy 75–7, 83
Ball, Lucille 157
Ballinger, Colleen 1–3
bandana, Harry's 40–1
Beachley, Layne 187
beliefs
  shared during workshops 196–9
  when feeling stuck 127–8
believe it or not lists
  fears 155–6
  feeling overloaded 69–70
  'not good enough' 38
  perfectionism 97–8
  when feeling stuck 127–8
  see also lists
Berlin, Irving 133
Bill, Emma's grandfather 136
book writing, making time for 8–9
'boundary ring' 81
bra incident 12–13
breakfast TV show 184–6
Brown, Brené 81, 107
Buddha 122
business see career and business
busy
  as 'badge of honour' 75–7, 83
  'hurry sickness' 4–5
  lack of time 3–4

C

D

E